Through the Eye of a Needle

Through the Eye of a Needle

A Story of Survival

Alec N. Mutz

with Brian Moore

iUniverse, Inc.
New York Bloomington

Through the Eye of a Needle
A Story of Survival

The views expressed in this work are solely those of the author and do not necessarily reflect the views
of the publisher, and the publisher hereby disclaims any responsibility for them.

iUniverse books may be ordered through booksellers or by contacting:

iUniverse
1663 Liberty Drive
Bloomington, IN 47403
www.iuniverse.com
1-800-Authors (1-800-288-4677)

Because of the dynamic nature of the Internet, any Web addresses or links contained in this book
may have changed since publication and may no longer be valid.

ISBN: 978-1-4502-5087-0 (sc)
ISBN: 978-1-4502-5088-7 (ebk)

Printed in the United States of America

iUniverse rev. date: 8/18/2010

For
My children—Andrew, Mitchell, and Nancy
And my grandchildren—Hannah, Samuel, Eliza, Gabriel, Isaac,
Gavin, and Brooke

In memory of Necha, Yitzchak, and Channah,
Three of the more than six million
Victims of the Holocaust

And for my father, Samuel,
without whom I would not have survived.
I still miss you very much.

Contents

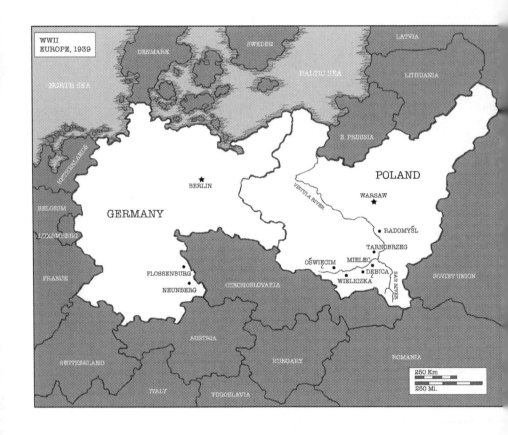

WWII
EUROPE, 1939

NORTH SEA

SWEDEN

DENMARK

BALTIC SEA

LATVIA

LITHUANIA

E. PRUSSIA

NETHERLANDS

BERLIN

GERMANY

BELGIUM

LUXEMBURG

FRANCE

FLOSSENBURG

NEUNBERG

CZECHOSLOVAKIA

POLAND

VISTULA RIVER

WARSAW

RADOMYSL

TARNOBRZEG

OŚWIĘCIM

MIELEC

WIELICZKA

DEBICA

SAN RIVER

SOVIET UNION

AUSTRIA

SWITZERLAND

HUNGARY

ROMANIA

ITALY

YUGOSLAVIA

250 Km

250 Mi.

1.

June 1942
Dębica, Poland

Hundreds of us huddle together in the crowded boxcar. In the train cars ahead and behind, thousands more. The air is heavy with the smell of excrement and hot with the screaming and crying of women and children. In the chaos, I can hear the voices of adults around me asking each other the same question—

"Was willen sie ton mit uns—What will they do to us now?"

The question goes unanswered. No one knows for sure.

Our journey lasts several hours before we hear the screeching of brakes. The cadence of the tracks beneath us slows to a halt. Someone outside approaches. The great metal door screams open to a scene that begins to answer the adults' question. We are not at a station. The train has stopped in the middle of nowhere, along a massive pasture. A sea of people like us—some still clinging to pillowcases filled with their belongings—sitting, waiting. Black-uniformed guards swinging truncheons, herding small groups of men towards a line of trucks on the pasture's edge.

Nazi officers appear below us in the doorway: *"Raus! Raus! Raus!*— Out! Out! Out! "

The crowd pushes together as it struggles towards the opening. Some jump from the boxcar. Others are pushed. Still others fall. All are ushered into the crowd of thousands. We walk past neighbors from Tarnobrzeg, their faces made less familiar by uncertainty, fear. Mothers try to comfort babies crying for milk after the long journey. Toddlers cry for food. We see the bodies of those who have already expired from the heat. SS guards shuffle past carrying large boxes of machine gun ammunition. They hurry as if a battle is raging nearby.

In the distance we hear the chattering of machine guns.

We stop a hundred yards or so from the line of trucks and are ordered to sit. I look at my *taty,* Samuel, my *mamy,* Necha. I see my brother, Yitzchak, a seventeen-year-old man, and my sister Channah who, at fourteen, is just two years older than me and starting to look like a woman. We exchange glances but say nothing.

We remain in the unbearable heat of the pasture for several hours. Nazi soldiers circle over us, selecting various men seated with their families. The men rise and are ordered towards the awaiting trucks, hurried along by swinging truncheons and screams of *"Mach schnell! Mach schnell! Verflucht Jude!*—Hurry up! Hurry up! Cursed Jew!"

A soldier stops at my brother, points, and makes a quick motion towards the vehicles. Yitzchak says nothing. He stands and walks quickly away, disappearing into the lines of men boarding a distant truck.

Not long after, we feel the shadow of another soldier over us. He lingers long enough for me to notice the sheen of his boots, the pistol strapped to his side, the glimmering SS insignia on his collar, the skull and crossbones on his hat. He points at my father with his truncheon and makes a quick motion towards the trucks. Taty rises and hurries away. He says nothing to Mamy. Nothing to me or Channah. Unlike Yitzchak, he is visible as he leaves us. He gets to the truck, puts his foot up on its back tire, and climbs up and over, into the trailer, and sits.

Mamy watches him as well. She begins crying, as does Channah. *"Du geht dan Taty,"* she says—"There goes your father."

And then, to herself, *"Du geht my man*—There goes my husband."

I can still see him sitting in the back of the trailer. I want to be sitting next to him. I don't want him to go away.

And then I do something I can't explain—I run.

I stand up and sprint towards him, away from Mother and Channah, past guards whose backs are turned and busy selecting other fathers and brothers, past neighbors and mothers and sisters and grandmothers and children who by now are beginning to understand what the Nazis are up to.

I get to the truck and put my foot on the wheel, just like I saw Taty do, and I struggle up and over the wooden side rails.

He sees me and is shocked, grabs me and sits me down next to him, says nothing. I look back and can still make out the faces of Mother and Channah amongst the thousands of others. I should have said goodbye to them, but it's too late now. I'm sure I'll see them again in a few days.

Taty speaks to me for the first time since our journey on the train began—"*Mir werden nisht deine mamy zehn nocht machl*—That's the last time you'll see your mother."

"*Nein! Nein!*" I cry. "*Mir werden sie zehn!*"—No! No! We'll see her again!"

As dusk approaches, the truck's engine roars and shudders to life. We pull away, and I find Mother and Channah once more and watch as they disappear into a mass of other faces. The crowd and the pasture fade into the dusk and the thick forest lining the road.

I can still hear Taty's words. I don't want them to be true. Surely, we'll see Mother and Channah again. Somehow, though, I know he's right.

2.

Life Before the War

As the truck makes its way into the forest, I think of my home in Tarnobrzeg, which now seems worlds away. I think of the monument of General Batory standing guard over the town's cobbled central square. I remember the storefronts. If I close my eyes, I can see my family's home, number 10 Broad Street, a whitewashed house with a tin roof that often conspired with the rain to keep us awake at night. I see the sign over the front door—"Ladies' Tailor Samuel L. Mutz." I can walk into the double front doors, into my father's shop, where he's studying sketches of dresses attached to the walls and making some of the best garments in all of Tarnobrzeg—dresses good enough for Count Tarnowski's wife, who would only wear Taty's clothing. He's holding a needle and thread up in front of me: "Do you want to see a trick, Alec?" He'd put his hands behind his back for a moment then bring them back out, the needle threaded and ready for sewing. When he finished with the stitching, he'd lift the great press off the fire and iron out every last crease and seam in his garments.

In my mind, I can leave my house and run down to the river Vistula, where the farmers brought their produce in every week for the public market.

And I can taste the blueberries.

Every now and then, Mamy would make pastries filled with wild blueberries picked from the woods surrounding our home. She would sprinkle the uncooked pastries with flour and sugar and put them on a tray, which I would take to the bakery on my way to school. At the end of the school day, when I picked them up, the cooked blueberries would be melted and running out onto the tray. I never made it far without taking a few bites.

By the time I arrived home, it was hard to conceal the crime. My father would look at me and say, "You clown—you look like someone painted your face!"

When I looked in the mirror, I saw that my mouth, teeth, and tongue were stained the same dark-blue color of the blueberries. No matter how hard I scrubbed, the color stayed. Only time would remove it. There were many days when I dressed up for synagogue and attended services with that blueberry-stained face.

I was a clown in more ways than this. Taty, who spent twelve hours or more each day tailoring, would often become frustrated with my behavior, as would other adults. Once, he took me to the doctor and waited outside while I was examined.

Inside the examination room, Dr. Pawlak questioned me: "How are you feeling, Alec?"

"Fine," I said.

"And how are the winds?"

The winds? I had no idea what he meant. What did the wind have to do with my health? Was he asking about the weather outside?

Dr. Pawlak grew frustrated, stormed outside and came back with Taty in tow.

"Mr. Mutz, is your son stupid? I asked him a simple question, but he will not answer me."

Taty leaned in close. "What did Dr. Pawlak ask you, Tulek?"

Tulek was a nickname Mamy and Taty sometimes called me.

"He asked me, 'How are the winds?'" I said.

Taty smiled. "He wants to know if you've been farting."

"What? He wants to hear me fart?" I was amazed that a doctor would ask his patient to do such a thing.

"No! No!" Taty said. "He wants to know if you've had gas lately."

Any other parents might have been embarrassed, but mine were used to my troublemaking. I once climbed into a tree and threw crows' eggs at my father when he told me to come down. Another time, a friend and I peeped on women who were changing their clothes in a bathhouse near the river. At Hebrew school, I grabbed a rabbi's beard in frustration and shook his head so hard that his yarmulke fell off. At home, I nearly swallowed a dead mouse as I drank from a pot Mamy was using to pasteurize milk.

Then there was the outhouse.

I heard from my friends that someone had set fire to a nearby outhouse, burning it to the ground. This was big news in Tarnobrzeg, so one evening, after I dressed in my holiday clothes for Passover celebrations, I snuck outside to explore the ruins. When I arrived, I saw the charred and still smoldering heap of boards where the outhouse once stood. I spent some time mulling around, kicking boards and climbing over the heap of debris. And then, as I climbed over one of the boards, I felt the ground fall from beneath me.

I suddenly found myself up to my neck in a pool of excrement. I floundered about, screaming for help and struggling to climb from the pit and the stinking mess it contained.

After I freed myself, I ran home as quickly as I could. I'm not sure whether Mamy smelled me or heard me first, but she met me before I got too far into the house. "No, Alec—you're not coming inside this house like that. Stay outside." She went away and returned with a metal tub, in which she poured water warmed on the stove. I stripped off my dirty clothes and hopped inside.

Taty came to the door and saw me getting into the tub and was shocked that his son was taking a bath outside, in clear view of anyone who might walk by. "What happened?"

Mamy gave him a look: "Do you even need to ask?"

"I fell into an outhouse," I said.

Channah saw me and ran from the house to stay with a friend until I was clean. Yitzchak shook his head. "You should have known better, Alec," he said, always the older brother.

Two of my friends walked by, laughing at me. "Oh—look at Alec. He stinks!" one said.

"Alec fell in the toilet!" said the other, before they both ran off.

Mamy spent more than an hour cleaning away the stench and filth that by then was caked on my skin. Slowly, my cleaner self emerged, and before long I was as good as new again, ready to find my next adventure.

I knew the ordeal was finally over when Channah returned from her friend's house. "Alec must be clean," she said to my parents. "It doesn't smell anymore."

Surprisingly enough, this wasn't my first experience with human waste. My Grandfather Wolf introduced me to its power a year or so before I fell into that outhouse, when he helped me with a problem I was having at school.

School was a one-mile walk from home. Every morning, Mamy would pack me a lunch of cheese or salami on a Kaiser roll, along with several snacks that would last me through the day. Our classes lasted fifty-five minutes, after which our teacher would send us out into the schoolyard to play while he prepared for the next lesson. I always used this time to grab one of the snacks from my lunch bag and eat. One day, when we returned from break, I discovered that someone had stolen my lunch. The next day, the same thing happened. And again the day after that. I finally figured out that Gedyn, the class bully, was responsible. When I told our teacher about the thief, he was unsympathetic, unable to believe that anyone would misbehave in his presence: "Someone stealing your lunch? That would never happen in my classroom."

When I told Grandpa Wolf about Gedyn stealing my lunch, he said, "Follow me." He found two pieces of bread and walked outside to the path the horses and other animals walked every day. On the ground were mounds of manure, one of which he picked up and brought inside. He placed the mound on one slice of bread, covered it with a slice of garlic salami, then with the second slice of bread. I couldn't believe my eyes. This was a first for me—I had never before seen a sandwich made from animal droppings.

"Take that to school tomorrow and leave it for this bully," Grandpa said. "He'll learn quickly."

The next day, I walked to school carrying the sandwich. I followed the same routine, leaving it in the classroom during break. Sure enough, the sandwich was gone when I returned.

Gedyn didn't look at me for the rest of the day. He sat silent, his face blazing red. And he never bothered me again. When I ran home to tell Grandpa Wolf about the victory, he didn't seem surprised, and I wondered if this was the first time he had made such a sandwich for a troublemaker.

While he did help me take care of Gedyn, Grandpa normally wouldn't hurt a fly. The houses in Poland were without screens, so during the summer, when the flies grew tired of the farm animals, they moved into the houses to pester us. He would eat his sour cabbage soup with clouds of them swarming him, alighting momentarily on his food before dashing off. Whenever I tried to kill them, he'd say, "Why do you try to kill the flies? What have they done to you?"

He was a poor milk salesman with a big heart. He would push his cart to the dairy farm every morning, fill his cast-iron milk containers, and push the cart all over town, delivering to all sorts of people. Unfortunately, most of the families would greet him at the door to tell him they couldn't afford to pay.

Grandpa would look at the desperate parents and their hungry children and say, "Well, take the milk now and pay me when you can."

After several days of delivering the milk for free, he would run out of money with which to pay the dairy farmer.

"Why can't you afford to pay for your milk?" my father would ask him.

"The families have small children, Samuel," Grandpa would say. "We can't let them starve."

Taty would then take money from his own earnings and pay the dairy farmer. And Grandpa would be in business for at least another week, before the whole cycle started again.

As kind as he was, however, he once tried to kill my father.

Taty served with the German army during World War One, until the Russians captured him, took him prisoner, and sent him to a labor camp in Siberia. When the war ended, the Russian guards overseeing the camp announced, "You're all free. The war is over." Nearly all the men stopped their work and ran off, even though it was thousands of miles to civilization and winter was close by. Taty decided to stay put until spring.

He survived the winter in Siberia, and when the snow began to melt, he headed west, walking for days at a time before happening upon a house or a farm, where he would work for food and shelter until ready to move on again. After more than a year and two thousand miles, he reached his family's house in Tarnobrzeg. It was the middle of the night when he arrived. The chickens and other animals were awakened as he approached, and before he had time to knock on the door, it swung open to reveal Grandpa Wolf standing in the doorway with an axe in his hands. "Get off my property, you thief!"

"Taty, it's me—Samuel."

"My son Samuel is dead—he was killed in the war."

"Taty, it's me. Look at my face. I walked from Siberia. I'm alive!"

Grandpa studied Taty's face. "It can't be you. We sat shiva for you. You're dead."

"Taty, it's me."

Grandpa looked at him for some time before he finally began to lower the axe, slowly at first, as if he was half expecting the man standing in front of him to pounce. They went inside, where Grandpa offered Taty milk and bread, which he ate quickly during brief pauses in telling his story of being captured, his labor in Siberia, and the long trip home. As each second passed, Grandpa realized that it was indeed his son Samuel sitting in front of him. He rose, put his hands on Taty's face and spent a moment studying him closely. Then, in a soft, quavering voice, he said, "My son, Samuel. I thought I would never see you again."

In the years that followed, Taty perfected his tailoring, found Mamy, and started a family. He never stopped working to support us. When he wasn't meeting with clients in the store or taking measurements, he was busy sewing. When he wasn't sewing, he was busy heating the heavy ironing presses. When he wasn't ironing, he was looking through books and magazines for the latest fashion trends. And when he wasn't doing any of these things, he was traveling around Poland, purchasing fabric.

During these trips to neighboring towns, Taty would gather the latest news and gossip from around Poland and the rest of Europe. Some stories he would hear from others. The rest he would get from newspapers, which he could read in nearly any language—Polish, German, Russian, Hebrew. It was in one of those papers that he learned of something called the Nuremberg Laws. He would come home from those trips and have hushed conversations with Mother, and every time I'd hear those words, always said in earnest—*Nuremberg Laws*.

When I asked Mother what they meant, she would always say, "You worry about what's important, Tulek. Be good in school. Be better than your seatmate. Be obedient. And be a good boy."

She'd then go back to cooking or tending to customers in the shop. Taty would go back to his garments. I'd go back to running around the streets of Tarnobrzeg, looking for adventure. And my world would return to normal.

The Jewish holidays were always special times for our family and the many others like us in town. Taty and Grandpa Wolf made sure that we carried out the traditions of all the holy days without exception. But even if it weren't for Taty and Grandpa, we still would have celebrated. Our house was only a short walk from the synagogue. Every Friday, just before sundown, the rabbi's assistant would make his way around town, reminding shop owners like Taty that the Sabbath was beginning. On occasion, we would see him enter the shop. Other times, we would just hear a voice from the doorway: "Samuel—it's getting dark. The Sabbath is beginning. Close the shop."

Taty never disobeyed. He closed his doors and prepared for the start of the Sabbath.

On holidays like Sukkot, Purim, Rosh Hashanah, and Passover, we would all dress in our best clothing and walk to the synagogue with the hundreds of other Jewish families who lived nearby. The women and girls all filed into an entrance that led to the balcony, while the men and boys entered another that led to the main-level seating.

I could never sit still through the services, many of which were between two and three hours long. After only a few minutes, I would start swinging my legs. Not long after that and I'd be talking to my friends, until Taty would lean over, grab my arm, and say, "Tulek, sit still and behave yourself." I'd manage to stay still for a few minutes before my energy got the best of me again. If I was lucky, I'd manage to sneak outside to see my friends.

The courtyard outside was always filled with children like me after an hour or so of each service. We always ran around, chasing each other, or we played a game that involved bouncing pennies off walls. It was great fun until I saw Yitzchak coming towards me. "Alec," he'd say, "Taty told me to drag you in by the ears if I have to. You have to come back inside."

By the time I sat back down, the women would no longer be seated in the balcony. They always got to leave service early so that they could go home and prepare the meals.

When we arrived back home, the table was always set for dinner. Dad, who always sat at the head of the table, started the meal with a prayer from the prayer book: "When God finished creating the heavens and earth, he blessed the seventh day and made it holy, because on it he rested from all his creative work."

On holy days like Passover, Mother brought the meal out in many courses, each of which had some significance that Grandpa Wolf explained to us. "The matzoh we are about to eat reminds us of how quickly our ancestors were forced to leave Egypt," he would say. "They had to collect only the possessions they could carry with them and flee. The bread they took with them did not even have time to rise. This is something we can never forget."

Later in the meal, Mother would bring out a plate of green herbs: "This is the maror," Grandpa would say. "We eat these bitter herbs on Passover to remind us of the many bitter years our ancestors spent as slaves in Egypt."

Our holiday meals went on for hours, with both Taty and Grandpa Wolf speaking and reading from the prayer book before each course. It was always difficult for me to sit still for such a long time, but I knew how special these times were, how hard Mamy worked to make the meal, and how important the prayers were to Taty, Grandpa, and the rest of our family.

Every now and again, a funeral procession would pass through Tarnobrzeg's central square on its way to the cemetery. As was the custom, the casket was placed in a glass-enclosed carriage, its black exterior so well polished that the light it reflected could blind you. Two beautiful black horses, heads nodding up and down in spasms as they struggled with their bits, pulled the carriage slowly along. Behind, a priest followed on foot, reading passages from the Bible. Half a dozen altar boys carrying crosses walked behind him, followed by a procession of relatives, friends, and neighbors.

I remember those of us who lived along the route—the old and the young, the healthy and the infirm, Jews and Christians—would stand outside in silence, men holding their hats in their hands, paying our respect to the deceased.

This was Tarnobrzeg before the Nazis came.

3.

Fall 1939
The Nazi Invasion

As hard as they tried to protect us from the news, my parents were unable to shelter us from word of the German army coming to take over our country.

It was September when I first overheard Mamy and Taty talking of the invasion. Soon after, they began mentioning the Polish army. Then we began hearing gunfire and explosions far off in the distance. Every day, the sounds grew louder. I pieced together clues gathered from my parents and knew that the Germans would soon arrive.

While many in Tarnobrzeg were fearful of what the Germans would bring to our town, Taty had a different opinion: "Let's just hope they defeat the Polish army quickly. Our army has no chance. The sooner the Germans win, the sooner life will return to normal for us."

He and Mamy had both heard of families escaping into Russia before Germany invaded. It seemed many thought Russia would be safer than Poland. Taty, however, refused to consider it. "We will not go to Russia," he would say. "We have nothing to fear with the Germans. Germans are a civilized people. The Russians are not cultured. They have no education."

He would often go to his room and return with a photograph of himself dressed in a German army uniform during the first World War.

"See this? Remember—I fought with the Germans in World War One. I was taken prisoner by the Russians and sent to a labor camp in Siberia. The Russians hate Jews. No matter how bad things get with the Germans, we're still better off with them than we are with the Russians."

So as the battle came closer and closer to our town, we waited, hoping for Germany's swift victory.

Several weeks after the invasion started, we began seeing Polish army forces in and around Tarnobrzeg. Since school never resumed after summer recess, I was free to spend my days spying on them from behind houses, horse carts, or anything else that offered me cover. On one of those days, I snuck into the town square and watched a Polish soldier driving a horse-drawn cart filled with pots and pans and crates of vegetables and other food. When he stopped, he began unloading the supplies and setting up a field kitchen.

As I watched him preparing to cook, I heard a sound unlike anything I'd ever heard before—a high-pitched howl that seemed to be coming from the sky. I looked up. The sky was cloudless, the sun shining brightly overhead. The howling grew louder and louder until I noticed a dark shadow cut across the sun.

The field kitchen exploded into a thousand pieces—a shower of onions and carrots and shards of wood falling into a smoking crater where a moment before all had been normal.

An aircraft screamed so close overhead that I ducked and ran for home. Along the way, I heard more explosions, saw houses on fire and billowing thick, black smoke.

I ran into the shop and told my father about everything I'd seen: "Taty! Taty! A bomb hit the field kitchen and blew it up, and houses are on fire!"

Mother came into the shop looking concerned. "You'd better keep him inside, Samuel," she said to Taty.

Taty turned to me. "Tulek, you must stay inside now. You'll be blown to bits."

But I didn't listen—there was too much to see to stay inside.

Several days after it started, the bombing and gunfire stopped. I ran from our house to the square again and heard a strange sound coming from somewhere in the distance, the sound of metal striking a rhythm on the cobblestone streets. It almost sounded like a horse's shoes clicking on the road, but this sound was louder, its rhythm more regular than horses—one, two, one, two, one, two.

This is when I saw them for the first time.

They marched in step, the metal cleats of their black-leather boots striking the cobbles in tight rhythm. Hundreds of soldiers, a great wave of uniforms, rifles, and helmets with strange, spider-like symbols on the side. Each man wore an emblem on his jacket—an eagle carrying that same spider symbol in its talons. And each wore a silver belt buckle with the same insignia: *"Gott mit uns—God with us"*

These must be good men if God is with them, I thought. They marched like an army that was protected by God. Not a single man was out of step. Each was healthy, well-fed. Uniforms were clean, boots polished. And there were so many of them. They looked like God's army.

The rumble of engines followed the men, and a wave of vehicles appeared—trucks pulling gigantic guns, motorcycles with sidecars mounted with machine guns. After the trucks, a band of uniformed musicians stopped in the square and began playing a marching song.

I stood there watching them for some time before I decided to run off and see what was happening elsewhere. I made my way towards the Christian monastery where, from several hundred yards away, I saw a group of German soldiers harassing a group of bearded men. The soldiers were shouting something, but I couldn't hear them from where I stood. One of the soldiers raised his rifle. I heard a shot and saw one of the bearded men drop. I had no idea whether the man was dead or just injured from the shot. I had never before seen such a thing happen. I ran home to Mamy and Taty.

"Taty! Taty! One of the German soldiers just shot a man at the monastery!"

Taty looked at me in disbelief: "No—they wouldn't do that Tulek. These are civilized people." He looked quickly at Mamy, whose eyes were wide with disbelief. "No, no, Alec," she said, "this is just what soldiers do. The man isn't dead. He just fell down." She and Taty looked at each other once again but said nothing else.

Not long after, we began hearing things in the middle of the night. First, boots marching through the nearby streets. Then fists pounding on doors and the screaming of *"Mach auf! Mach auf!—Open up!"*

Then the crashing of furniture against walls, glass shattering, people screaming.

The sounds frightened me, and I ran into my parents' room, where Mamy and Taty were always awake and waiting. "Don't worry, Alec. This will end soon," they would say as I fell asleep.

Within a matter of days, a group of five Nazi officers barged into my father's shop. Mamy, Channah, Yitzchak, and I hid while Taty dealt with them. It was the start of Yom Kippur celebrations, so Taty was wearing his prayer shawl. The officers were dressed differently from the soldiers I saw marching into town—they wore green-grey uniforms with "SS" pins on their collars.

One of the officers approached my father, looked at his prayer shawl. "Look at this—we have a Jew here," he said.

Another walked to Taty's tailoring table and began opening drawers and rifling through his belongings. One of the drawers was particularly interesting to him. He reached in and removed a big pair of scissors, the kind Taty used to cut heavy fabrics. "And what are these doing here?" the officer said.

"I'm a tailor. I use them for my work."

The soldier's expression changed. He approached Taty and without warning pushed him down on the work table. He held the scissors to Taty's stomach and looked at the other soldiers. "Why don't we cut this Jew's belly open and see how he bleeds?"

Mother held her hands to her face and gasped when she heard this. There was silence in the room for what seemed an eternity.

"We have a lot of Jews in town," responded one of the officers. "And we have plenty of time to see how they bleed. *Lass ihm laufen*—let him go."

The soldier with the scissors released his grip on my father. He threw the scissors on the floor, turned, and left with the rest of the group.

Taty's face was pale. He was a big, strong man who feared no one. Never before had I seen him frightened. When we were sure the Nazis were gone, Mamy, Yitzchak, Channah, and I returned to the shop to be by his side. "Let's just hope they don't come back," he said.

They did.

Two days later, an army truck stopped outside the shop and soldiers armed with machine guns poured out. Two stood guard outside while several more burst in. They pointed their guns at Taty: "Whatever is in this shop now belongs to us!"

Taty stood silent as the soldiers took all of the beautiful material he had so carefully selected for his fall-season garments. They took his press irons, his scissors, his sewing machines—everything. They didn't waste a moment. In an instant, everything was piled in the truck, and the soldiers were off to rob the next shop.

"Well, there goes our livelihood," Taty said to Mamy. "But I'll get more material for next season. All will be well." We heard his words but could see on his face that he believed otherwise.

In September, less than a month after we first learned of the German invasion, the posters went up—

Jews are hereby ordered to report
With personal belongings to the
market square before noon on 2 October.

Taty, Mamy, and Yitzchak packed all they could into a suitcase. Channah and I were given pillow cases, in which we packed underwear, socks, and other clothes. Grandpa Wolf arrived at our house with his belongings as well.

We left during the morning of October 2nd, Mamy, Taty, Grandpa and Yitzchak carrying their suitcases, Channah and I our pillowcases. The streets outside our home were crowded with a procession of families like ours, all carrying their belongings and walking in earnest towards the town center. There was little noise as we walked. Mamy, Taty, and others like them had been told this was a resettlement of the town's Jews. The Germans led us to believe there was nothing to fear.

When we arrived, the town square looked unfamiliar to me. Once each week, farmers would come in to sell their goods and the square would become crowded with people. But the crowd we saw on this day was larger than any I had ever seen. I had no idea there were this many people in all of Poland, let alone in Tarnobrzeg. Thousands upon thousands were crammed together, all holding onto whatever belongings they were able to carry. Nazi soldiers watched as groups of people arrived. They ordered all older people to a far corner of the square, everyone else to lines leading to long tables. The square sounded nothing like it did during farmers' markets. All was silent except for the cries of children and the shouting of the soldiers who watched over us.

We waited in line for some time before we made our way to one of the tables. Several soldiers stood behind it, several more in front. One of them looked at Channah and me: "You two—empty your pockets!"

We had nothing. They moved to Mother, Yitzchak, and Taty and patted down their arms and legs, felt their pockets for hidden objects.

"Put your bags on the table!" another officer shouted.

We followed his orders and watched as the soldiers behind the table rifled through our belongings as if they were looking for something. They found nothing of interest in my pillowcase. But as they searched Taty's suitcase, they came upon a small pair of tailoring scissors Taty found after the soldiers robbed his store. They threw them into a box. In Mamy's, they found her favorite cameo and threw it in with the scissors. I could see the sadness on her face when they took it. Taty had bought it for her as an anniversary gift. It was beautiful—deep beige with diamonds sparkling on its surface, it hung from a white-gold chain. It was a stylish and expensive gift that Taty worked very hard to afford. He saw Mamy staring at it in the box. "Don't worry, we'll get another one," he said to her.

The officers returned our belongings and motioned to a corner of the square separate from the one where the old people were sitting. For some reason, the soldiers didn't send Grandpa off to wait with the older people, so all of us joined thousands of others and sat, waiting, without food or drink, until the sun started to set. Just as my hunger was becoming unbearable, Mamy reached into a pillowcase and grabbed a loaf of bread, which we shared. All around us sat people my family and I had known for many years. I saw schoolmates, rabbis, Hebrew school teachers, all wearing similar looks of fear on their faces.

On the other side of the square, soldiers ordered the elderly people onto a horse-drawn wagon. It pulled away, and not long after, we heard machine gun fire off in the distance. When the wagon returned, it was empty, ready to start the process again.Within a matter of hours, none of the older people were left.

4.

Radomysl, Poland

N ear dusk, the soldiers ordered us to our feet. "You are to walk to the town of Radomysl," they said. "Do not stop until you arrive."

We walked through the night, until my legs grew so heavy that each step felt like a kilometer. After several hours without stopping, I began to weep, and Mamy and Taty encouraged me as best they could. "We'll be there soon, Tulek. Then you can rest," they said.

Daybreak revealed the Polish countryside. Radomysl was nowhere in sight. The road was lined with the remains of trucks and busses bombed out during the invasion. We walked through the morning, and with the afternoon came dark clouds and a downpour that refused to end. It saturated us and our belongings, making my pillowcase so heavy that I could barely carry it. The road turned quickly to ankle-deep mud so difficult to walk in that we huddled under trees to wait for the rain to subside. But before long, the Polish police, whom the Germans ordered to escort us to Radomysl, pointed their rifles at us and ordered us to move along. I was surprised that our country's own police would help the Germans remove us from our homes.

We continued on. Occasionally, peasants from nearby towns would offer us hope that we would someday arrive. "Continue on this road," they'd say. "Radomysl is not far now."

On more than one occasion, however, awaiting peasants took advantage of the crowd's weaker members, robbing them of the few possessions they carried. An entire family was robbed as they sat down

19

to rest. Another man, whose belongings were draped over his bicycle, lost everything as well. He told us after that he had lost more than his bicycle and clothing: "Before we left Tarnobrzeg, I cut the bike's frame apart and hid gold pieces inside. The person who stole it will probably never know."

After two and a half days of walking, we reached the river San, which we crossed using a crude bridge made of wooden planks. Just before my family crossed, a woman who was pushing her twin babies in a carriage slipped off the slick boards and fell chest deep into the river. The current was so swift that she nearly pulled the baby carriage into the river with her. "Help!—Please help!" she cried. The men standing near her reached down and pulled her to safety just before she was swept away.

On the other side of the San, Radomysl finally appeared. Because the Nazis had sent so many of us here, there were few places to stay in the town itself. Our only option at first was a hay barn. Then Taty managed to find an inexpensive room with a stove and a kitchen. We were all excited to move from the barn, but our excitement faded when we discovered that the room was infested with lice, bedbugs, rats, and just about every other vermin imaginable. Mamy told Taty that the place was uninhabitable. "We'll all get sick in this place, Samuel."

"You're right," Taty said. "But we must stay here until we find an alternative."

That small room was our home for the next three months. Taty had managed to sneak a needle, thread, thimble, and another small pair of scissors past the soldiers in Tarnobrzeg, all of which he put to use, performing alterations and repairs around town in exchange for food and other goods. In order to escape the packed room and the rats, I spent much of the time exploring Radomysl, which was much smaller than our town. It did, however, have a soda factory, which a local Jewish family owned. I walked in the front doors one day and became fascinated by the machines that filled the bottles with carbonated water and sent them to a man who flipped the caps down and locked them. After observing for several minutes, I walked up to him and said, "That looks easy. I can do that." He looked at me and said, "You think you can do this? OK—go ahead and try."

I sat in front of the bottles and quickly mastered the art of locking the cap on each. The man was surprised. "Well, you're good. How old are you?"

"Nine," I said.

"Good. Why don't you come back tomorrow and work?"

I ended up working there three hours a day for many weeks, closing so many bottles each day that my hands would ache. When I wasn't capping, I was loading the bottles into wooden crates and stacking them for delivery. It was hard work. But at the end of each week, I would be paid several zlotys, which I would run home and give to my family.

Mamy was always impressed: "You're such a go-getter, Tulek. We're so proud of you."

I was proud of myself as well. Channah always helped Mamy with the chores. Yitzchak was an apprentice and helped Taty with the tailoring. And now I helped as well, even though I was the youngest in the family. Grandpa, however, did little. He often told us that he missed his milk cart and the families he delivered to. His whole life was gone now, he said, and he spent most of his time sitting silently, staring.

Many of the Jews my father came in contact with in Radomysl planned on migrating east to Russia. They saw this as the fastest way to get their families to safety. And safety to them meant being as far away from the Germans as possible. The subject came up often between Mamy and Taty, but it never became a discussion. Taty still refused to consider leading us to Russia. Instead, he proposed the opposite: "We must go west," he said. "My cousin Froyem Kornbluth and his family live in Mielec. We can stay with them until we are allowed to go back home."

When I heard his plan, I thought of the posters I had seen displayed all around Radomysl—

Jews are not to be
Seen outside
From dusk to dawn.
Anyone seen outside
During these hours
Will be killed.

We knew that Polish police worked with the German army to make sure we stayed here as ordered. But this did not seem to worry Taty.

A week later, he told us to pack our belongings. "We're leaving tonight," he said, "and we won't be walking this time."

That night, Taty led us down to the river San, where a man was waiting for us with a small rowboat. We got in. Taty handed him five zlotys he had saved from his tailoring and the man took us to the opposite shore, where a horse and wagon were waiting for us. "We're going to Mielec," Taty told the driver. The wagon lurched forward and continued for several hours. Morning came, and I could see concern on Mamy's and Taty's faces. Every person we passed along the road seemed to make them anxious. It was several hours after daybreak when I realized why they were so concerned.

The wagon slowed to a halt in front of a group of German soldiers standing in the middle of the road. "What's this?" one said. "Where are you headed, and who has given you permission to travel?"

Taty responded in fluent German: "My name is Samuel Mutz. I served with the German army during World War One and was taken prisoner by the Russians and sent to Siberia. We have heard that the Vistula River will be the new border between Germany and Russia. I want to keep my family as far from Russia as I can. We are headed west to Mielec, where we will join relatives."

His confident explanation satisfied the officers, who waved us on.

We were stopped several more times before reaching Mielec, and each time Taty's explanation satisfied the soldiers enough to allow our journey to continue.

By late that afternoon, we had reached Mielec. Unlike Radomysl, Taty was familiar with the city and directed the cart driver to his cousin's house, where Froyem ran out to embrace us.

"My cousin Samuel!" he said. "Please, please, bring your belongings inside—quickly, though. My house is open to you and your family."

Inside, Foyem updated Taty on the situation in town.

"Things are not well here, Samuel. Mielec is now a full-fledged ghetto. Our movement is restricted and things are getting worse by the day. My daughter, who was a talented gymnasium student, cannot attend classes at school any longer. The German armed forces are headquartered at the school now. She has been ordered to clean toilets, polish boots, and wash floors for them. Last week, when she did not report to clean, soldiers came here to order her back to work.

"And on Rosh Hashanah, when the women went to the slaughterhouse to slaughter their fowl, soldiers locked them inside and set fire to the place. They burned—all of them. Many others are dying each day. Just look outside—their bodies aren't even cleared away. They're left on the street like animals."

Growing up in Tarnobrzeg, I had seen dead farm animals from time to time. I pictured people being left out like those animals and became saddened. Why would anyone want to do this? Farmers cleaned up their animals, so why wouldn't someone take the people away to bury them? This made no sense to me.

Taty did not respond. He only continued listening silently.

"Samuel, I've heard of many families going to Russia—far away from the Germans. We should go, and we should go soon."

Finally, Taty spoke: "No—I will not take my family to Russia. All this will pass."

Froyem had no choice but to accept Taty's response. "If you stay, you must know that all Jews are ordered to wear the Star of David. We'll have to make them for your family."

Taty cut our stars from yellow fabric and sewed them to our garments, and for the next fourteen months, we stayed in Mielec. Taty tailored for many of the Nazi soldiers, and the rest of us tried to stay inside and out of trouble. I hated being inside all day and often found myself exploring the ghetto, where thousands of Jewish families like ours tried to live life as normally as possible. This was difficult when we had to wait in line for something as simple as a loaf of bread. Often, the women would wait for hours, only to learn that the baker had run out. "But when will you bake more?" they would ask.

"I do not know. It is difficult to find flour these days," the baker would say. And so the women would disperse until the next day.

I soon grew so tired of the boredom that I stopped by the gymnasium and asked a group of German soldiers for a job. "Well look at this," one of them said, "a little Jew who has volunteered to work." He went inside and returned with a shovel and broom. "Here—you can sweep. Report back to me at the end of each week."

I swept the gymnasium every day. The soldiers always seemed to have plenty of alcohol to drink. They would drink and sing patriotic German songs as I cleaned, getting louder and louder as the hours passed—

> *Wenn der Sturmsoldat ins Feuer geht*
> *Ei, dann hat er frohen Mut—*
> When a stormtrooper goes into battle
> He has cheerful courage.

I would keep my head to the ground, sweeping and scrubbing intently so they would not know I was listening.

> *Und wenn das Judenblut vom Messer spritzt*
> *Dann geht's nochmal so gut, dann geht's nochmal so gut—*
> And when the Jewish blood splashes from a knife
> Then everything is going well, everything is going well.

The first time I heard them, I ran home to tell my father. "Taty! Taty! The soldiers are singing a song about killing Jews with their knives!"

For a moment, he did not respond.

"They don't mean that, Tulek. The Germans are a cultured people. These are just army songs the soldiers sing," he said.

But the longer we stayed, the more I realized that the soldiers were not just singing songs. Every so often, I would go outside and walk past the body of someone whom the Nazis had executed. Sometimes, a small crowd would gather around the body. Other times, it seemed no one noticed. Whenever I saw them, I thought about how the people once walked and spoke and had families like mine. They used to sit down with their families for meals, and now there they were, in the gutter with hundreds of people walking by. If those people could be executed, then so could Mamy, or Taty, or me.

It was the first time in my life that I thought about dying. I wanted more than ever to go home.

It was Taty's tailoring that finally allowed us to return to Tarnobrzeg. The Nazi soldiers he worked for in Mielec liked his work so much that he was able to negotiate a travel permit allowing us to go home. We packed what little remained of our belongings, said goodbye to Froyem and his family, and hired another wagon for the thirty-five kilometer journey home.

Four or five hours after leaving Mielec, Tarnobrzeg appeared in front of us. We realized as we got closer that the place we had left no longer existed. As our wagon moved slowly into town, we were greeted with flattened buildings and unfamiliar faces. No one we knew was left. Soldiers occupied the market square. Most of the houses we passed were occupied by strangers. *Volksdeutchen*, Taty called them—people of German ancestry. The unoccupied houses were burned out or robbed of their windows, doors, and other belongings.

Our house still stood. It looked no different from when we left it more than a year earlier. Taty's name still hung on a sign over the front door. But through the windows we could see that another family had moved in.

When Taty saw this he ordered the driver to continue on.

Yitzchak, Channah, and I protested: "But Taty, this is our house!" we said. "They can't take our house from us! It's ours!"

Taty's simple response was difficult for us to understand: "A German family has moved in. We have no choice." He turned his back to us and said nothing more.

We stopped at a house without windows and doors. Taty walked inside to see if anyone was living there. When he reappeared, he told us this would be our new home. We unloaded our belongings and went inside.

During the next several weeks, Taty and Yitzchak found doors and windows, which they had installed in the house. Taty was able to begin tailoring again, and our new life in Tarnobrzeg began to take shape.

While my parents did their best to make this new house our home, my favorite place quickly became the town church, where I was able to get a job pulling weeds in the gardens and orchards. I worked there every day, and each time I arrived at the church I was greeted with a "Good day, Eliahu!" from Father Pius. He was very old, perhaps eighty-five, and he would always be wearing a white robe and carrying his Bible with him. As I worked, I would see him walking through the gardens, reading, his lips constantly in motion in silent prayer. When he grew tired, he would sit on a garden bench and pray, sometimes for hours at a time.

I loved talking with him. He always called me by my Hebrew name, Eliahu, and always asked me questions about life and the teachings of the Torah and the Bible. Since I had not been to school in a year, I valued every one of our conversations. "You should always learn, Eliahu," he told me on more than one occasion. "Never, never stop learning. You should always strive to learn more than you know. Children can absorb knowledge like a blotter."

Once, he began speaking to me about what the Bible tells us about Abraham. "Abraham?" I said. "But Abraham is a Jew."

Father Pius smiled understandingly: "You're right, but he is Christianity's prophet as well. You see, Eliahu, Christians and Jews are one and the same in many ways."

Never in my religious studies had I learned that Jews were like Christians.

As I left church that day, Father Pius gave me something to do when I got home: "Pray for this war to end soon, Eliahu, and for Poland to become an independent country again."

"I will, Father," I said. "I'll see you tomorrow."

I returned to church the next morning to find Father Pius lying in a pool of blood on the ground. Above his body, posted on the wall, was a notice—

This priest was accused of being
an active member
Of the partisans and has been
Executed by order of
General Keitel

For what seemed like hours, my eyes moved from the sign to his body, then back to the sign. I thought of our discussions, of how peaceful and kind a man he was, of how gently he walked the gardens, of his lips constantly moving in prayer. And I thought back to the first time I saw those words on the German soldiers' belt buckles as they marched into town—

Gott mit uns

It was then that I realized God could not be with the Germans. God would never support people who would do such a thing to such a gentle old man, to a priest who devoted his life to God.

I ran home to tell my parents. "Father Pius?" Taty said. "How could Father Pius have been a member of the resistance?"

Mother could say nothing through her weeping.

That same week, a group of men carried an unconscious man with a bloody and swollen face into our house. It took us several minutes of looking at him to realize it was Yitzchak. He had been clearing debris from the railroad tracks when one of the German officers began beating him. They left him for dead outside. Had it not been for the men who brought him to us, he most certainly would have died.

No sooner had he been nursed back to health than we were ordered to a vacant lot alongside the old cemetery, where soldiers forced the remaining Jews in town to march to the town of Baranów. We began walking just as we had before, only this time German soldiers and Polish policemen marched alongside us. They wove their way in and out of the crowd, removing the older members of the group. One of them pulled Grandpa Wolf away from us. The soldier walked him to a tree, put a pistol to his head, and pulled the trigger.

Grandpa dropped to the ground.

Mamy cried hysterically—"How can you do this? How can you do this? He is an old man! He didn't harm anyone!"

Yitzchak and Channah cried also. "Why? Why?" they asked Mamy and Taty.

Taty remained silent. He had survived World War One and knew about death.

I looked behind me at Grandpa's body, which lay motionless on the ground. The Polish police forced us to continue marching, and before long I could no longer see him. I thought of the bodies on the streets of Mielec and again of the animals sometimes left in the fields after they died. And I felt the tears run down my face as I thought of my grandfather—a man as sweet and gentle as Father Pius—being left at the side of the road.

Hours later, we arrived in Baranów, where we stayed for several days before being ordered to the railhead, then onto boxcars that took us to the field near Dębica where I ran to join my father on the truck that is now driving us to an uncertain future.

5.

June 1942
Tarnobrzeg, Poland

We are mostly silent as the truck bounces along the tree-lined road from Dębica. Many of the men around us sit with their heads down in prayer. Over the roar of the engine, I hear men contemplating their fate—

"We'll surely be killed."

"Do you think they'll kill us now, or use us as laborers?"

Taty breaks his silence and says, "I hope they are not going to murder your mother." Then, after a moment, "I wonder where Yitzchak is right now."

I can see the sadness in his face. "At least we're together, Taty," I say. But he doesn't seem to hear.

Not long into our journey, we start to notice familiar landmarks through the dusk. At first, a farm, then a pasture, then a group of homes.

"Look," one of the men says, "that's Dr. Pawlak's house. We're headed back to Tarnobrzeg."

He's right. We soon find ourselves in the middle of town, surrounded by familiar buildings and places. The truck stops, and when we are ordered out, we find ourselves standing in the rabbi's sanctuary—a large courtyard surrounding the temple and house where our rabbi lived at one time. I know this place well. My brother was friends with Rabbi Horowitz's son, and I sometimes followed Yitzchak and his older friends to the courtyard to play. He always grew frustrated with me and tried to send me off, but I always managed to stay with him anyway.

The place at one time had beautiful grounds and gardens maintained by a staff of the rabbi's workers. Now, the gardens are gone, trampled by passing soldiers. The temple itself has been stripped of its ornaments and converted into an auto-repair garage. All around the perimeter, men strain to lift large, wooden poles into deep holes in the ground. Another group of men are busy unrolling sections of barbed wire and attaching them to the poles. At the sanctuary's entrance stands a guard's house, where an armed German soldier stands with his German Shepherd.

"*Raus! Raus! Raus!*" soldiers scream, pointing their guns at us. "Get into line. We're going to count you."

We fall quickly into line, where I stand next to my father. The soldiers walk past us counting, then go back to the start of the line and start again. They repeat the process once more before meeting together for a moment. They then turn to two approaching men—a Gestapo officer and a civilian with a cane in one hand and a cigar in the other—and say, "We have 101 here."

"101? Are you certain you've counted correctly?" the man with the cigar says.

"Our count is accurate."

"I only have permission from the government to have 100 men here," the man says, removing a letter from his pocket and holding it up to the soldiers.

The SS officer turns to the line and walks to us. He examines each of us before stopping at me. "What is this little Jew doing here? He can't work on the crew. He'll be wasting food."

No one answers.

"It's no matter," he continues, "I'll be back tomorrow to take care of him."

The other soldiers lead us into a storage shed where the rabbi kept wood and coal for his home. Straw has been spread on the floor, where we will sleep until morning. Just before I drift off, Taty says, "Don't worry, Tulek, you'll be fine."

At dawn, we awaken to the shouting of the guards—"*Raus! Raus! Raus!* Roll call!"

We rush out into the courtyard and line up. The man with the cane and cigar returns. He is wearing riding britches tucked at the knees into his socks, and I notice today that the hand with which he holds his cigar has only two fingers. The SS officer returns as well and waits for another soldier to count us. When the soldier reaches the end of the line, he says, "100."

He recounts.

"We have 100 today."

"Well, then," the man with the cigar says, "I have my 100 men. Take them off to the road."

Then he points at me. "And this little Jew will be good helping in the kitchen. Take him there."

Taty tells me later about the rumor he heard. One of the original prisoners escaped the sanctuary during the night. The police found him sitting along the Vistula, executed him on the spot, and dumped his body into the river.

Taty and the rest of the men are led out of the sanctuary, and I go to the kitchen where another prisoner—an older man—assigns me my duties. "You are to feed the pigs and clean the sty. Each afternoon, you are to bring the soup out to the road crew." He points to a four-wheeled cart with a forty-gallon wooden barrel on top. "The soup will go in the barrel, and you'll bring it to the men. When you're done with all of those jobs, you'll help rinse pots and split wood for the stove."

Later that afternoon, the cook calls me over. He empties a great pot of cabbage soup into the barrel on the cart. I wheel it out to the guardhouse, where the guard opens the gate and accompanies me out on the road. I pull the heavy cart for an hour before we reach the men, who are busy hauling and dumping sand and rocks for the new road. Three or four Ukrainian guards and the man with the cigar watch over them. Taty and the rest of the prisoners look exhausted. By the looks of it, they have been working non-stop since dawn. The filth of the road clings to them.

As soon as they see the cart, they drop their tools and line up for soup. Most carry small, tin bowls and spoons hooked onto their buttons. There's pushing and shoving for places at the back of the line, where it seems most of the men want to be. As I ladle soup into their bowls, I understand why—all of the cabbage and carrots sink to the bottom of the barrel. Those at the end of the line get more solids than those at the front.

After the men eat, I wheel the cart back to the sanctuary and work at feeding the pigs. I'm given fifteen kilos of potatoes, which I place into a large steamer. I fill the steamer with water and start the fire, and thirty minutes later, I return to remove the freshly steamed potatoes. When I smell them I realize how hungry I am. I glance around to be sure no one is looking and place two in my pocket. They are warm against me as I dump the rest of the load into a trough and add corn, rye and milk. The more ingredients I add, the more I think of the cabbage soup I just fed to the men. I use an iron masher to beat the mixture into a thick soup, which I then scoop into a bucket and bring to the pigs. The moment I enter the sty, the pigs squeal in anticipation of their meal.

When the men return that night, we are counted and moved to the synagogue. Straw has been dumped alongside the walls, and this is where we sleep.

Taty is exhausted from working on the road since dawn. I take the potatoes from my pocket and offer one to him. He takes it and eats it quickly, but it seems to do little for him. "It's going to be difficult to survive this for very long, Tulek." Then he is asleep.

During roll call the next morning, the man with the cigar makes an announcement: "My wife needs a tailor. Is anyone here a tailor?"

Taty speaks up immediately—"I'm a tailor."

"What kind of a tailor?"

"I'm a women's tailor. I owned my own shop here in town before the war started."

"Come with me," he says, leading Taty off.

That day, as I work in the garden, I hear a woman's voice calling to me. "Alec," she says. "Alec!"

I follow the voice to the fence, where I see Mrs. Wróblewski, a woman who often used to come in to Taty's shop for garments and fittings, standing on the other side.

"Good morning, Alec," she says.

"Good morning," I say.

She pulls a jar of raspberry syrup from beneath her apron. "I have something for you."

She rolls the jar under the fence and turns quickly to walk away before anyone sees her. I take the jar into the sanctuary and hide it where Taty and I slept last night. All I want to do is sit and stare at the syrup, but I know I have to get back to work before someone sees me.

As I haul the soup out that morning, Mrs. Koza, another woman who knows my family, calls to me from her house along the road. The guard allows me to run over to her house, where she hands me three hard-boiled eggs and another jar of raspberry syrup. I get back to the cart and the guard takes the eggs from me and eats them. He then takes the syrup and pockets it.

I am anxious to tell Taty about the food when he returns that evening, but he tells me about his day first.

"The man with the cigar is Hans Hoffman. I knew of him before the war started. His family moved from Germany, and I've done some work for his wife before. I worked at his house all day. He told me today that he, too, fought for Germany during World War One. 'Samuel,' he said, 'we both know that you Jews are to blame for Germany's loss during the last war.' He walked over to a framed picture of Adolf Hitler and spoke to it: 'Adolf—you had to take us into Russia. And now we'll get our asses handed to us.' He turned to me after he said this. 'You never heard me say that, Samuel.'"

Taty then takes a small sack of bread from his pocket.

"He handed this to me and told me that we'd have separate quarters in the synagogue for me to do tailoring for his wife."

This is good news for us. We've only been in the synagogue for a day, and already we know that the rats and vermin are a problem. We move to a small room that might have been an office for one of the rabbi's helpers before the war. Taty has barely enough room to tailor, but we are thankful that we are away from the rest of the prisoners.

I pull the hidden jar of syrup from its hiding place to show Taty, then I tell him about the soldier stealing another jar and eggs from me.

"What?" Taty shouts. "How can you let him do that?"

"But what was I supposed to do?"

"Eat it! Eat it, if you know what's good for you. They can't take it from your stomach after you've eaten it."

33

At morning roll call days later, the soldiers count 101 of us again. They double and triple count until they conclude that the number is accurate.

"We have 101 today—how can this be?"

A man steps forward from the line. "I am the extra man. My name is Abe Warchowski. I was being held at Camp Rzeszów, but I escaped to come here to be with my father."

The soldiers confer with one another until the SS officer says, "Very well—you will stay here while the rest go off to work on the road."

Hours later, I and two other prisoners are ordered to find shovels and report to the courtyard, where a group of policemen, SS, and soldiers stand waiting near Warchowski. We walk out of the sanctuary, through town, to a forested area near the river, behind the town brewery. We stop. The police officers look at us and point at the ground, where we dig for the next hour until a two-meter-deep hole is left in the ground. We pause to look up at the soldiers, and one of them says, "Make it deeper."

One of the police officers looks at Warchowski as we continue digging: "Do you smoke?"

"Yes," Warchowski says.

The officer hands him a cigarette and lights it.

Warchowski is pale faced as he smokes, his hand trembling when he removes the cigarette from his mouth.

"Hop in," the police officer says.

Warchowski hops down and stands in the hole, facing away from us.

"Kneel down."

Warchowski obeys.

The policeman takes a handgun from his holster and fires twice. Warchowski's head snaps forward and his body goes limp, slumps facedown in the grave.

The policeman looks at the body for a moment, then turns the gun to me. "Those look like good pants on him—jump in and take those pants off him."

I hop into the grave and wrestle with the still-twitching body to get his pants off. When I'm through, I struggle to climb out of the grave.

"Now cover him up," the policeman says.

L ater, Hoffman finds me in the kitchen. "I need you to help me send some things off. We're going to the post office."

I spend the next several hours packing honey, preserved pork, and other produce into straw-filled wooden crates, which I then stack on my cart. Hoffman tells me to follow him, and I wheel the cart out of his house, onto the main road heading into town. I pull the cart in the road's gutters while Hoffman walks on the sidewalk. We were told earlier that Jews always had to walk in the gutters.

Not far from the post office, we see a Gestapo officer walking towards us on the opposite side of the road. As soon as he sees us, he crosses the street to confront Hoffman.

"What are you doing with this Jew here?"

"We're doing highway construction," Hoffman responds. "I'm part of the Berman Construction Company. I have Jews working here. I'm their supervisor."

"You have this—this piece of filth Jew—for construction? He's worthless for construction. He's wasting food. Why don't you let me take him out into the forest? I haven't killed a Jew in two or three days."

"If you kill him," Hoffman says, "I'll have to take a man off the road crew to work in the kitchen. I need to keep him."

The Gestapo officer becomes suspicious. "Are you a member of the Nazi Party?"

Hoffman reaches into his pocket and produces his Nazi Party credentials. "Of course, are you?"

"Of course," the officer says, producing his papers. "Well, if you have any sick Jews or loafers who aren't willing to work, let me know. I'll be happy to take them out." He snaps his arm up in a salute and says, "Heil Hitler!"

Hoffman returns the salute and says, "Sure, I'll let you know."

When the officer is at a safe distance, Hoffman continues: "What an idiot." But I don't respond. I never know whom to trust.

W eeks after we arrive, the lice and vermin infestation in the temple becomes worse. Men die every day while out working. Others die in their sleep. I walk into a barn and find the body of a man who must have died days earlier. The rats have found him and are crawling all over his body. I grab a shovel in the barn and raise it over my head to beat the rats off. But I don't want to hit his body as well, so I lower it to the ground.

I run to get my cart and ask a shoemaker named Hirschel Hirschorn to help me lift the body onto it. When we lift, the rats cling to him, still gnawing. We push the cart away and spend an hour or more digging a grave near the camp's fence, then heave the body inside. Still, the rats stay with him. There are dozens of them in the grave with him, moving busily from his eyes to his nose and ears. I start shoveling dirt on top of him and the rats try to scatter, but I continue until I can see only dirt.

I wheel my cart back to the kitchen, where the cook is working at cleaning the decomposing carcass of a goat. The stench it carries is unbearable, and its skin is alive with thousands of maggots.

"This is all right," he says to no one in particular. "I can clean it up and mask the stench with cabbage. They'll still eat it. No one will ever know."

Hours later, he serves it to the prisoners.

I wake up not long after, shivering with a fever. Taty manages to get me out for roll call, then returns me to the small room where he tailors. I'm too sick to work in the kitchen. My fever worsens throughout the day, and I close my eyes and drift off. When I awaken, Taty is sitting next to me and places a cold cloth on my head. "You'll pull through, Tulek." I drift off again.

I awaken to Taty saying, "Tulek—Tulek, I have something for you." I feel the cold metal of a spoon on my lips and taste a warm liquid with a sweetness I haven't tasted in many years. "It's Mrs. Wróblewski's raspberry syrup, Tulek." Then he fades away.

For several days, I awaken to the syrup, and slowly, gradually, my fever breaks and I regain enough strength to sit upright. Taty is relieved. "I think it was typhus, Tulek. You're lucky."

Then, "It was Mrs. Wróblewski's syrup that pulled you through."

Many others do not pull through. And the sickness is not limited to the prisoners. The animals have begun to die off. As I prepare the pigs' food one afternoon I find several dead piglets in the sty. Just then, Hans Hoffman walks in and sees them and comes at me swinging his fists. "This is your fault, you worthless Jew. You haven't kept the sty clean enough. I'll teach you never to forget to keep this place clean." He shouts and punches at the same time. Three or four of the blows knock me to the ground. Then, as quickly as it starts, he's gone.

I hate Hoffman for beating me. I hate him for blaming me for the pigs' deaths, when it's his fault for the filth of the entire sanctuary. I hate him for caring about his pigs more than the men building his road.

The largest pig in the sty—a sow—walks by, and I take a shovel and slam it down as hard as I can on its hind legs. It sounds like a human screaming as it runs away, and I can see that it is lame—the blow has damaged its legs. It will surely die soon.

Back in our room, I tell Taty about Hoffman beating me. His reaction isn't what I expect: "Well, at least he didn't kill you. When I tailor for him, he always gives me a piece of bread to take to you. Try to remember that."

For just a moment, I feel bad about the sow. It only wants to live, just like the rest of us.

There is an SS officer whom we always see driving around town drunk. We see him through the fence racing through the streets, tires squealing as he negotiates turns. He sometimes tears past me as I'm wheeling the cart out to feed the men.

One afternoon, two police officers order me and an older prisoner to follow them to the police barracks in town. They lead us to the garage, where inside we find the mangled body of the SS officer lying on a wooden plank. Dark, dried blood cakes his hair, which stands on end like a porcupine. Bruises cover his yellow skin, and his arms and legs are twisted in impossible ways.

"He hit a tree in his car this afternoon," one of the officers says. "We're going to have a torch parade for him this evening before his burial. Clean him up and dress him in his uniform." He points at a folded uniform in the corner of the garage.

When the officers leave us, the other prisoner says, "I wish this would happen to more of them. Maybe then they'd get the message."

We stand staring at the body for a moment before he continues: "We'll need boiling water to straighten his limbs and get the blood off."

We gather wood and start a fire, over which we boil a large pot of water. After cutting his clothes off, we pour the hot water over his joints, then struggle to straighten them. All goes according to plan until we get to his hair, which is tangled with dried clots of blood.

"We'll pour boiling water on his head—it's the only way to clean it."

When we pour the water over his head, his hair starts to come out in clumps. I take a comb and begin combing it back, only to see even more hair coming out. We panic—"He'll be bald by the time we're through. They'll kill us! We can't send him out for the parade without any hair."

But there is nothing we can do until we begin dressing the body and find an SS officer's cap to place on his head. No one will see his hair at all.

The police return with a horse-drawn wagon draped in flowers. Torches blaze from each of the wagon's corners. We help lift the body on and watch them head off towards the cemetery.

The next day, as I bring soup out to the men, we pass by the cemetery and the guard overseeing me orders me to begin taking care of the soldier's grave and those of three others. "You're to wipe the gravestones clean every other day and keep them looking respectable," he says.

The first gravestone is decorated with an army helmet with a bullet hole through it. I clean it up and move on to the drunken officer's grave. As I approach I see that the gravestone has a pile of human excrement on it. I kick the pile away with my feet and move on.

In the middle of a night like any other at the rabbi's sanctuary, we are awakened by barking dogs and soldiers with machine guns screaming, "*Raus! Raus! Raus!*"

They are all SS troops this time, and we are rushed into an awaiting truck. I look around at the other men inside once we are all on board. There are only thirty-five of us left.

As the truck pulls away from the sanctuary, Taty says, "This is probably the end."

6.

June 1943
Mielec, Poland

There is no conversation in the truck. The only light comes from the motorcycles in front of and behind us, each with a sidecar mounted with a machine gun.

The truck pulls away from the rabbi's sanctuary and drives for several hours before it stops and we are ordered out. The sun is just beginning to rise, shedding enough light for us to see several large hangars, buildings that look like barracks, all surrounded by two barbed-wire fences.

"Raus! Raus! Raus!"

We are familiar with the routine by now—we are ordered to fall into line for counting.

Several armed SS officers stand next to men dressed in unfamiliar blue uniforms. We later learn that these men are *kapos*—Jewish prisoners who help to keep the camp in order. Most of the kapos are volunteers who hope that maintaining order for the Germans will get them more food. It does not take us long to realize they are as brutal as the rest of the guards.

We are ordered to sit on the ground and await instructions. Behind us, I manage to catch a glimpse of three electricians attaching large wires to the metal of the fence. In front of us, a tall man in civilian clothes walks to the SS officers and has a brief conversation with them. While they speak, a short SS officer walks up to the group. He seems important. The other men turn to him and stop speaking when he arrives. He carries a black riding whip under his arm, and speaks to the group for a moment before walking to the electricians behind us.

The tall man in civilian clothes then walks to us and speaks: "I am Mr. Bitkover. My wife and I are prisoners here like you. You are now in Concentration Camp Mielec. The camp is overseen by Commandant Schwammberger." He points at the SS officer with the riding whip. "You will be employed in the airplane factory, where each of you will be assigned a job in a different area." He pauses and points to two buildings behind us. "You will stay in these barracks. You should go there now and find a place to sleep. Work starts promptly at 6 am. You will need to be up earlier if you want a slice of bread."

Just before we stand up to go, I turn to hear Commandant Schwammberger still speaking to the electricians: "Have the fences been electrified?"

"Yes, Commandant," one says, "we have just finished."

Without warning, Schwammberger pushes one of the electricians backwards and into the fence. There is a large pop followed by the loud hum of electrical current. The man convulses for a moment, smoke drifts from his back, then he drops to the ground.

Schwammberger nods his head in approval, turns, and walks off.

The barracks are filled with rats and the stench of body odor and excrement. Four tiers of wooden bunks line the walls, some of which are occupied by men who have recently returned from the night shift. Our group awakens them with our questions.

"Is anyone in this bunk?"

"Is anyone sleeping in this one?"

Finally, one of the resting men explains the simple system to us: "If there's no one in it now, it's yours. And if someone is in that bunk when you return from your shift, find another."

Taty and I climb to a bunk next to several men who have just gotten off the night shift, which is 6 pm to 6 am. Taty sees that they are not yet asleep and asks them about the factory work and camp life.

"You will be making parts for aircraft," one responds. "They will assign you a job and train you tomorrow. Get up before 6 am for bad coffee and a slice of bread. They will march you from the factory for lunch, which is always cabbage-and-potato soup. You will have no other breaks until they march you back at the end of your shift."

Another man adds, "And never, never go to the dispensary. You can only stay there for two days. On the third day, the wagon will come for you. When they take you out on the wagon, only your clothes return."

We are counted the next morning at 6 am, and one of the soldiers says, "We need tailors to repair prisoner and officer uniforms. Is anyone here a tailor?" This is the second time Taty's tailoring might help us.

Taty raises his hand and is led off to a small room next to the barracks. The rest of us march to one of the giant hangars. At the entrance a Ukranian kapo takes me to a machine and says, "You'll be working here." He shows me what I will do from dawn to dusk every day. I am to go to the lathe to pick up boxes of unfinished screws and bring them back to my machine, where I will place each screw into a chuck and lower a small blade down on its head, creating the slit used to turn the screw. When I'm through with the entire box, I am to bring it to a vat of acetone for cleaning.

The job becomes monotonous after a short period of time, and I quickly become covered with the grease spray that lubricates the blade of my machine. But as I look around at the other prisoners, I realize how lucky I am—nearly all of the others are on their feet for the entire day. I get to sit on a stool in front of my machine; I am allowed to take brief lavatory breaks when I need them. Over the next two days, I learn that in order to conserve energy, it's best to work slowly until the kapos walk by to yell at me.

At the end of my shift, I walk through the barracks to find Taty, who is in a small shack filled with ceiling-high piles of prisoner uniforms. His job is to repair holes and clean stains from executions, then fold the uniforms and distribute to those who need them. I walk to the shack every day after work and spend hours sleeping on the piles of clothing and talking to Taty. Because he sees so many people throughout the day, he always has the latest rumors about happenings around camp. But often, our talks turn from rumors to Mamy, Channah, and Yitzchak.

"I wonder where they are, Tulek," he says. "Are they being tortured? Are they alive?"

These are questions I cannot answer, but I try: "They're probably working at another factory like this one."

"I hope so, Tulek," he says.

At the end of every shift, we are marched from the factory in rows of four. Guards wait for us, counting, under a larger iron sign that hangs over the factory entrance—

Konzentrationlager Mielec
Nebenstelle Auschwicz
Concentration Camp Mielec
Satellite Camp of Auschwicz

One day, I am the last person in my row. As we near the sign, I see an SS officer holding a wooden club, counting us—"196, 197, 198, 199…"

He looks at me, and as he says, "200," he swings his club. It crashes into my arm and the worst pain I have ever felt runs through me. I can do nothing but continue marching.

When I get to Taty's shop, I tell him what happened. He takes my left arm and moves it gently in his hands, and pain shoots through my body. I can hear the crunching of bones and see the swelling. I know I'm hurt badly.

Just then, Taty sees Mr. Bitkover walking by outside. He runs out and brings him in. "My wife is a doctor. I will bring her in to examine him," Bitkover says, looking concerned.

He returns with his wife, who takes my arm in her hands, examining it gently. "It's shattered," she says.

"What should we do?" Taty asks.

Dr. Bitkover finds two small boards in the shop and ties them around my arm with scraps of clothing from the uniforms. Her husband asks Taty for a long-sleeve jacket, which Taty quickly finds. When I put the jacket on, the sleeves cover the splint completely.

"He must keep this jacket on at all times. He cannot let the guards see the splint. Fortunately, his fingers are just fine. He'll be able to continue working without any problems," Dr. Bitkover says. Both she and her husband smile and walk out.

Three weeks later, I remove the splint, and my arm is healed. I think of what a kind woman Dr. Bitkover is. But before long, we begin to hear rumors that her husband talks down to the Commandant, that he will surely be killed soon. Not long after the rumors start, we hear four gunshots while marching back to the barracks. At the camp entrance, we see Mr. Bitkover's body lying outside of the electrified fence. Across the road is his wife's. Blood drains from two bullet holes in their heads.

I run to Taty's shack to tell him what I've seen, but he isn't surprised. "I already know," he says. "Several Ukrainian guards just came in to drop off uniforms. They told me what happened."

It is October 1943. We have been in Concentration Camp Mielec for four months.

Those in our barracks are ordered to line up in front of a table, behind which sits a drunken Ukrainian guard. He is holding a large needle, which he dips into an ink well. "Hold out your wrist," we hear him saying to each man who approaches the table.

The men obey, and I watch as the guard jabs the needle into their wrists. Occasionally, he dips the needle into the ink well, then goes back to stabbing. Each man who walks away has two dark, bleeding letters on his wrist—*KL*. I learn later this stands for *Konzentrationlager* and is meant to identify us as prisoners.

I am second in line for my tattoo. The man in front of me approaches the table.

"Are you married?" the drunken guard asks the man.

"Yes."

"And where is your wife?"

"I don't know where she is."

"Let me see your ring finger," the guard says.

The man holds his left hand out.

"No ring. Where is your ring?"

"They took it from me before we were sent here," the man says.

The guard laughs to himself, dips the needle into the ink well. "Then I will have to give you another."

He holds the man's hand down and stabs a crude line of ink around his ring finger. "There, now you have a new ring."

The guard dips the needle again, stands up, and etches a Star of David into the man's forehead. "And there—now you're a proper Jew."

He waves the man away and looks at me. My legs move me toward the table. I have no time to think, no time to be scared. He tells me to hold out my wrist and spends several minutes etching a small *KL* into my wrist, then sends me off. When I get back to the barracks, my wrist is bloody and swollen. The pain only goes away when I get to the factory and lose myself in the monotony of the slitting machine.

Not long after, I awaken shivering, shaking, goosebumps and a rash all over my body. Taty knows prisoners in the kitchen and manages to boil some water and finds potato peels for me. He heads off to the shack for work, then comes to see me later.

"Tulek, you must go to the dispensary. If you don't show up for work, they expect you to be in the dispensery. If Schwammberger finds you here, he will kill you."

I remember what I've heard about the dispensary. I think of the men taken away in the wagon, of their clothes returning for Taty to mend.

"I can't go to the dispensary, Taty," I say.

"Tulek, you must—it is the best thing to do for now."

I obey him and walk to the dispensary, where inside I find a row of beds covered with straw-filled burlap bags. An attendant sees me and points at a bed. "You can have that one," he says. "They just took him out several hours ago."

As I lie down, I can see fleas jumping and bed bugs dropping from the ceiling. The man in the bed next to me says, "Looks like the bedbugs have declared war on the lice. We'll see who wins."

I stay in the dispensary for two days. No one attends to me, except for a prisoner who brings me bread once a day. I understand quickly that this place is not meant to help heal prisoners. It's a holding pen for those who need to be executed.

A man named Dr. Birk walks in every morning with several kapos and soldiers. He points at men and says, "Him...him....him," and the soldiers grab the men and take them out to the wagon.

Dr. Birk knows my father works as a tailor and goes to see him at the end of my second day in the dispensary. "He'll be taken out tomorrow," he says. "Tomorrow is his third day."

Early the next morning, before dawn, Taty sneaks into the dispensary, picks me up, and carries me on his back to his shop, where he buries me under one of the large piles of clothes. I sleep until I'm awakened by the angry voice of a man yelling at Taty.

"We're missing a little Jew," he says.

I can tell it's Commandant Schwammberger—I've heard his voice many times before.

"We think the little Jew is your son. Where is he hiding? Is he in here?"

Taty says nothing.

I hear the loud crack of a pistol firing and feel quick movements in the clothes covering me. Then footsteps walking away. Then silence.

Taty rummages around in the clothes until his face appears in front of me, white with panic. "Are you hit?"

"No," I say, "I'm fine."

I stay in the pile of clothes for another day before I'm well enough to return to work. Surprisingly, the kapos at the factory say nothing to me about the past several days. I sit down at the slitting machine and go back to work.

The next time Schwammberger enters Taty's shop, it's for a different reason. He hands Taty the uniform of a dead SS officer, along with a pair of silver epaulettes. "I want you to make my son an SS uniform. He is eight years old. You will come to my house to take his measurements."

A few days later, when the uniform is finished, Taty is summoned back to Schwammberger's house. His wife and mother-in-law look on as Taty dresses the child in the uniform. It fits perfectly.

"You've done an excellent job," Schwammberger says to Taty. He walks to a closet and takes out a pistol and holster, which he hands to his son. "Fritz—you can now come with me and I'll teach you how to kill Jews. I'll take care of the big ones, and you can have the little ones."

His wife interrupts him: "Josef, what are you doing to him? He's only a child. He has plenty of time to learn how to kill Jews, but not now."

Schwammberger becomes irate. He draws his gun and points it at her face. "What kind of a Nazi Party member will he be if he does not know how to kill Jews, you filthy Jew lover?"

He opens the front door and calls to a guard, then points at Taty. "Take this Jew back to where he came from!"

I am on my way to visit Taty after work when a wagon carrying potatoes drives by on its way to the kitchen. It hits a bump and several potatoes fall out. I and an older prisoner run over to take them from the ground. Before we know it, two SS guards are on us—"What do you have there?" they say.

We hold the potatoes out to show them.

"You filthy swine of a Jew. You're stealing food from the camp," one of them says to me. He hits me several times in the face, and when I fall to the ground I feel his boot crash into my mouth, my head, my sides. I scramble up off the ground and run off as quickly as I can. When I glance over my shoulder, I see that both of the guards are now on the other prisoner. They drag him to a wall, tie his hands behind his back, and hang him from his arms. He screams out in pain.

Just before I reach Taty's shack, I see Commandant Schwammberger walk by the guards. He looks briefly at the man they're torturing and says, "You're doing an excellent job," then continues on until he passes another prisoner heading to work at the factory.

"Stop right there, you filthy Jew," he says.

The man stops in front of him at looks and the commandant.

"You looked at me, you Jew. You're still looking at me."

The prisoner looks quickly at the ground.

"Don't you understand that I am your god? You don't look into the face of god."

He pulls his pistol out and fires. The prisoner hasn't yet fallen to the ground before Schwammberger has holstered his weapon and moved on.

When Taty sees me, he is surprised. My front teeth have been knocked out, and I am covered in blood. But when I tell him what happened, he is disappointed "You know better than to be doing that, Alec. You know better."

It is July. I am fourteen now.

We begin hearing the sounds of heavy artillery outside the camp. Rumors follow quickly—the Russians are moving in. The German army is being defeated. We'll be free soon. I think of home and the rest of my family. If the war ends soon, maybe we will all have survived.

There are railroad tracks that run through the factory, and one morning a train rolls in towing a line of empty boxcars. We don't report to work that morning. Instead, armed guards with dogs order us into the cars. The doors are closed behind us and once again I am standing in a train crowded with other prisoners.

Taty and Mamy's wedding photo, 1924

Taty's shop, 1936. To his left is my cousin, Rosi Fleischer. Years later, Nazi soldiers threatened to cut his belly open on the table seen at right. Mamy, Yitzchak, Channah, and I hid behind the fabric partition in the background.

Taty's shop, 1938. Left to right: Taty, Yitzchak, Rosi Fleischer, and two shop helpers. Dad could make garments just by looking at them. Notice the pictures over his shoulder and the heavy press on the right.

Channah, Taty, and Yitzchak

49

Yitzchak and cousin Rosi Fleischer

A view of Camp Flossenbürg

When Taty saw this picture of me in the uniform, he said, "Guns never solved a thing in the world, and look at you showing it off."

Mrs. Rossman's house on Austrasse Street. Taty and I stayed here after liberation. I later visited while stationed in Germany.

51

Phyllis and me after my graduation from Rochester Institute of Technology.

I'm standing at the station where Dad and I were unloaded before being marched to Flossenbürg.

This is a view of K.L. Flossenbürg, taken during my 1995 trip to Germany with Mitchell. Nazi soldiers and kapos would keep the stairs icy. Prisoner who slipped and fell were beaten or killed.

Me with Representative Louise Slaughter at a 1998 remembrance ceremony, Washington, D.C.

A recent photograph of Phyllis and me

The Mutz family, 2008. Front row (left to right): Hannah, Jennifer, Nancy, Gabriel, and Phyllis. Back row: Andrew, Samuel, Gary, Mitchell, Eliza, Alison, Isaac, and me

7.

July 1944
Wieliczka. Poland

We stand in the boxcars for the next four hours, and for the entire time we hear the sound of heavy artillery close by. "Well, our hope is not in vain," someone says. "They have met their enemy, and the end is close."

"If the fighting is that close, we may survive and soon be free!" another says.

When the train stops, the door opens and we find ourselves at the train station for a town called Wieliczka. Guards order us off the train and we are lined up and counted, then marched away from the station to another camp surrounded by barbed wire. As we walk beyond the fence and into the camp, I can see it's almost identical to Mielec—prisoners in stripes, barracks with no windows, high fences. I look around and notice that some of the guards from Mielec have followed us here. The only difference seems to be the lack of aircraft hangars.

We are lined up and counted once again, then sent to the barracks to find bunks for the night. The place is filthier than Mielec. Several bodies lie in the corner. The stench of sweat and urine fills the air. As we climb up to inspect the bunks, we notice that the wooden planks we are to sleep on are spaced two or three inches apart. From the top bunk, I can see all the way to the bottom. A few of the boards are covered with straw, and these quickly become the ones men fight over.

That evening, as we try to sleep, we hear the voices of guards outside. They laugh and sing until we hear one of them say, "So how many Jews can we kill tonight?"

A machine gun chatters outside and we hear bullets shredding the thin wood walls of the barracks before the gun goes silent. The guards' laughter outside fades as they walk away.

The next morning at roll call, one of the guards smiles and says, "So how many did we get last night?" Two prisoners are ordered to run into the barracks and carry out the dead. They enter and come out with a body. They enter again and bring out another, then another, until there are five bodies on the ground. One of the bodies is still twitching until a soldier fires his pistol and it is motionless.

We are led to elevators that take twelve at a time down to our work. When we leave the elevator, we look up and see that we are in the bottom of a salt mine, its walls rising up several hundred feet above us. The elevators are the only way in and out. The mine's floor is covered with equipment and machines, many of which we recognize from the airplane factory. But none of the machines are operating. Many are completely covered with rust. Most of the prisoners are either sitting down or sleeping, and the guards don't seem to care that no one is working.

"There are no materials for us," one of the prisoners explains. "The Germans are against the ropes and have run out of materials for their war machine. Even if they had materials, they'd be useless here. Look at these machines. The moisture and salt in this pit make them useless."

Taty looks at me and says, "This isn't the worst place for us to be, Tulek. At least they'll leave us alone when we're in the pit."

After twelve hours without work, we are put back in the elevators and marched back to the barracks. That evening, we hear more singing outside, followed by more machine gun fire into the barracks. I am so tired and hungry that I no longer fear the bullets. The hunger is painful. When I manage to doze off for a few minutes at a time, I dream of home and the fat blueberries that grow all over town. Morning comes slowly, and the hunger is even worse. Soldiers drag a wounded man out during roll call. A bullet grazed him and he is bleeding, but he is still alive.

"Please! Please! Don't kill me! I want to live! I want to live!"

One of the soldiers straddles him and takes out his pistol, aims it at the man's head.

"Please! I want to live!"

"Yea, yea," the soldier says before firing twice into the man's head.

We stay in Wieliczka for three weeks until they march us back to the station and put us back on the box cars. The sound of heavy artillery exchange echoes all around us. For the next three days, the train starts and stops. Occasionally, the door opens and someone slides in slices of bread and a bucket of water, and we can see a train station or a field outside before it closes again.

Finally, we come to what seems to be our final stop. Outside, we hear guards, and above us, through the open top of the car, we can see smoke stacks billowing a thick smoke. A smell unlike any other I have experienced hangs in the air. The door opens and we see soldiers, another barbed-wire fence, and a sign—

Konzentrationslager Auschwitz
Arbeit Macht Frei
Concentration Camp Auschwitz
Work Will Free You

Soldiers slide bread and water inside and tell us to move the dead to the doorway, where a man wheeling a cart of dead prisoners collects them and wheels away to the next car. As he takes them away, I see their arms and legs and heads bouncing on the cart.

Taty sees me watching and says, "They're not in pain anymore, Tulek. They have suffered enough."

A soldier approaches to close the door. He points at a pair of tall smoke stacks inside the camp, each of which bellows a thick smoke that hangs in the air around us. "Don't worry, you'll all be liberated soon—through those stacks." He smiles at us as he slams the train's door closed.

Men around us begin to speculate: "Auschwitz—this is the Germans' killing machine. This is the end."

We stay in the boxcar for several days, eating a slice of bread and drinking a few sips of water every day, sleeping on our feet or, if we're lucky enough to be in the right place, by leaning up against the walls. Men collapse and we move them to the doorway for collection.

Taty and I make our way to the front of the car, just below a small, rectangular opening in the wall. Taty crouches down and I stand on his back to get some fresh air and a look outside. Our car is the first behind the train's engine. I can see an SS officer with grenades hanging off his belt climbing up to the conductor and yelling, "We have no time to gas them, let alone incinerate them. Take this rubbish away from here!"

Hours later, the train begins moving.

It has been eleven days since we left Auschwitz. The train stops often and waits for hours at a time before continuing. Men die every day, unable to survive on bread and water alone.

For brief moments here and there, Taty loses hope. "Let's get this over with," he says. But just as quickly he begins wondering about Mamy and Channah and Yitzchak, and he is hopeful that they are still alive and well.

Every time they open the door to feed us, we catch glimpses of the war—destroyed villages, bombed-out houses, twisted train tracks. One afternoon, we stop in the middle of nowhere, alongside a lake. Soldiers order us off the train and allow us to clean ourselves. Those who are still able run to the water and jump in. We scrub ourselves and our clothes and drink before being called back to continue the journey.

A day later, our journey on the train ends. The doors are opened, and we see that we are at the railroad station in the German village of Floss. We are ordered off the train but are too exhausted to worry about where we will go next.

8.

August 1944
Flossenbürg, Germany

From the train station we are marched five miles to our next camp. Mountains consume the skyline all around us. As we enter another camp surrounded by barbed wire, we pass beneath two stone guard towers connected by a stone bridge. Soldiers stare down at us from behind machine guns. A sign overhead says

Konzentrationslager Flossenbürg
Arbeit Macht Frei

Once inside, we see that the camp is massive—what seems like hundreds of buildings, all surrounded by tall stone towers occupied by guards with searchlights and heavy machine guns.

We are ordered to sit on the ground in a paddock in a corner of the camp. "You will be quarantined here until your barracks has been cleared out," one of the officers says. We stay seated for hours before they bring us bread and water. The bread crumbles into a powder in our hands, and clouds of sawdust fall to the ground. The hot August sun beats down on us until night brings the freezing mountain air. We shiver until sunrise, huddled close together for warmth.

When the sun has risen over camp, I notice a mountain of eyeglasses in a corner of the courtyard. Other men see it as well and begin to wonder: "Who did those glasses belong to? And where are they now? What happened to them?"

"I hope our eyesight holds out and we never need glasses," Taty says.

Off in the distance, in the center of the courtyard, a Nazi flag flies on a large flagpole and soldiers beat prisoners who are passing by.

We sit out in the open for two weeks before soldiers lead us to barracks number 22. For the first time, the barracks is completely empty when we arrive. Later, we learn that all of the men had been done away with hours before we were ordered to enter. "The Germans work us until we are too weak to move. Then we're no longer useful to them and they send us to the smoke stacks," someone says. Throughout the day, we hear a rumbling off in the distance, echoing off the mountains like thunder. Overhead, the faint sound of aircraft becomes louder and louder, until a wave of planes passes far overhead. We see a glimmering cloud dropping from beneath them—light reflecting off something they're dropping. We watch the cloud descend for several minutes before a few small strips of metal land in the camp. "Aluminum," one of the men near us says. "They drop tons of it to throw the Germans' radar off."

I look up again and see birds flying overhead, almost as if they are in formation with the bombers. They land on the fences surrounding us, on the barracks' roofs, then flap their wings and fly off, into the hills around us, away from the camp. It strikes me how effortlessly they come and go, and I find myself wanting to be one of those birds. If only I could flap my wings and be away from this place.

Another wave of bombers passes overhead shortly after the first, the planes' wingtips so close that they seemed to be glued together in formation, blocking out the sun for moments at a time as they pass. A wave of thunder echoes through the mountains.

"You see—we very well might make it yet," one of the men says. "The Americans and the British are bombing the Germans. This is the end."

That night, I hear another wave of planes flying overhead, followed by more thunder. I wonder if he is right.

A loud whistle blows to wake us for roll call every morning and we follow a crowd of men outside to the camp square. Often, after we get outside, we notice that a gallows has been brought in and placed next to the flagpole. Guards bring out men, women, and sometimes children to be hanged. Sometimes the men are wearing tattered uniforms. Sometimes they are naked. Some have been beaten. The guards who oversee the executions always mock those about to die. And the children always weep as the nooses are tightened around their necks. "Shooting them would be too painless," someone says. "The Nazis want a show. And with the Allies coming closer and closer, they can't afford to waste their bullets."

One of the first men we see hanged is wearing a Russian officer's uniform. Guards lead him up the steps of the scaffold and order him to stand on a chair while they pull the noose over him and tighten it down. Just before the guard reaches to pull the chair from beneath him, the Russian looks at us and yells something in a language I cannot understand. I ask Taty what he said: "He was speaking Russian. He said, 'My only sin is that I'm a Russian general. Long live freedom!'"

On another day, the guards bring out a man, a woman, and two children. The children cry as they are prepared—"Why? Why?" they say.

One of the guards looks at the children and says, "Because your father is a traitor, and you'll be a traitor if we let you grow up."

The children continue crying until the chairs are pushed from under them. The only thing I feel as I watch is hunger.

We are moved to barracks number 10 just as winter arrives at Flossenbürg. Taty and many of the other men have been assigned to work at the quarry. I tell a kapo that I operated the slitting machine at Mielec, and he takes me to a hangar, where I'm ordered to operate a drill press, drilling holes in thin sheets of metal. When we get back to the barracks in the evening, it seems as though the Germans are running out of room for us—the barracks is crowded with what seems like a thousand or more men. We stumble over each other and have no room to turn when we sleep. The stench from the filth and the dying is stronger here than in any of the other places we've stayed.

There is a set of stone steps that we often have to walk to get from place to place. For entertainment, the soldiers sometimes hose them down until they are frozen solid. They wait at the bottom with guns and truncheons, and when prisoners slip at the top and fall to the bottom, the soldiers laugh and beat them, sometimes to death. Whenever I see them waiting at the bottom, I take off my wooden clogs and walk down barefoot to give myself better traction. Fortunately, I never slip.

Shoes are more important here than at any of the other camps. Without shoes or the clogs the soldiers sometimes provide us, our feet are torn to shreds. At night, we guard them, keeping them under our heads as we sleep, or tying them around our wrists.

Taty wears a pair of black leather shoes that he laces to his wrist as he sleeps at night. I wake up one morning to the sound of him saying, "My shoes—my shoes are gone," and I see him searching frantically around his bunk. I try to help find them, but they're nowhere to be found.

"Someone cut them off my wrist last night. Help me find rags and some wire. I need something on my feet."

We find a rag, a burlap bag, and two thin pieces of wire, and Taty is able to make crude coverings for his feet. "It'll have to do," he says after he finishes.

I walk up to one of the kapos overseeing us and tell him that someone stole Taty's shoes.

"His shoes, stolen?" he says.

"Yes, someone cut them off his wrist last night while he was sleeping."

"Find the man who is wearing them, if you can. Then let me know who he is."

I watch the feet of every man who passes me on his way to get food, examining each pair of shoes for the black pair Taty was wearing. Finally, a man walks by wearing a pair of black shoes that don't even fit his feet. His heels hang out over the ends and he shuffles awkwardly as he walks in them. When I look closely, I immediately recognize them as Taty's shoes.

I run back to the kapo: "That man there—those are my father's shoes."

"Him?" the kapo says. "He's a Russian—I'll show him."

The kapo picks up a heavy, three-legged stool, walks up behind the Russian man, and smashes it down on the man's head. The man drops to the ground, bleeding, twitches for a moment, then is still.

"Take your father's shoes and give them to him," the kapo says.

I obey. When I hand the shoes back to Taty, I tell him about the kapo and the stool.

Taty is not thankful. "You had a man killed for my shoes?"

"I didn't have him killed. I just told the kapo he was wearing them."

"That's not right—that man should not have died for my shoes."

He sits for a moment in silence before he puts them back on his feet and all is back to normal. "They feel lighter," he says. "I could dance in the ballet."

Each day Taty returns from the quarry, he looks thinner, more exhausted. The thin soup and sawdust bread we eat every day is not enough to keep him going. He is looking his worst ever when we run into Yitzchak Seiden—a man from Tarnobrzeg who knows Taty well. When he sees Taty, he is saddened by his appearance. "I work at the factory building wooden crates and receive a food ration every day. I will bring you something to eat. You look weak."

The next day, Yitzchak returns with food. Taty eats and seems ready for another day at the quarry.

Just when we think it can get no colder, the mountain air surprises us. By the middle of winter, the cold at night is unbearable.

I begin to have difficulty swallowing. After several days, I can barely eat because of the pain. On my neck, I feel a lump that grows larger every day. Taty tells me it's a boil and tracks down a prisoner who was a doctor before the war. The doctor looks at my throat, feels the boil. "I don't have anything sharp enough to drain it. I work as an orderly at the dispensary, but they don't allow us to have knives. He'll have to have this looked at by the doctor."

The next morning, I walk through the snow to the dispensary. Just inside the entrance is a sign—"No Shoes"—with many pairs of shoes piled beneath it. I remove my clogs and walk into a large room lined with a single bench and a number of rooms and cubicles that orderlies are entering and leaving. The bench is lined with prisoners waiting for treatment. They are much worse off than I am. Many look like skeletons who are about to die. All of them have a black number painted on their foreheads.

A doctor wearing a white coat over his SS uniform comes out of one of the rooms, followed by two orderlies. He stops in front of me long enough for me to see the name written on his jacket—Dr. H. Schmitz. Around his neck hangs a necklace with a small ink pot hanging from it. He looks at me for a moment, then removes a small paint brush from the ink pot and paints a number on my forehead. He walks off and into another one of the rooms.

As I wait, I begin to watch the orderlies walking from room to room and from cubicle to cubicle, their white jackets stained with blood. One leaves a room carrying a leg by the foot and I can see a bloody mess near the thigh where it has been cut. The orderly opens another door, places the leg inside, then walks to another cubicle.

Well, Alec, this is it, I say to myself.

An orderly comes out and points at me, then at one of the rooms. "Go in."

When I enter the room I notice the stench and a gurney covered with dried blood and other filth. I climb up and lie down. Dr. Schmitz enters. He looks at my neck for a moment before swabbing it with some kind of a liquid. "*Messer bitte*—knife please," he says to the orderly.

The orderly hands him a scalpel and the doctor slices into my neck. I feel a quick pain, followed by the warmth of a river of blood. The orderly swabs at the blood, until the doctor turns and leaves the room without saying a thing. I can feel the blood pouring out of my neck and I think of the rest of the prisoners waiting outside, of the leg the orderlies carried out. I get up and walk as quickly as I can to the entrance, stopping for a moment for my clogs, which are gone. I have no choice but to run back to the barracks in my bare feet.

When I get back, I find a faucet dripping cold water and rinse the wound as best I can. It's then that I remember the piles of garbage that the guards leave around the camp, and I wonder if there's something there I can use to help the bleeding. I run outside and find one of the piles, on top of which sit several empty concrete bags. I grab one and run back to the barracks, where I tear the bag into thin strips. The strips are still covered with dust from the concrete, and when I tie one around my neck, the dust absorbs the blood and forms a crust. Slowly, the bleeding stops.

Outside, a body collector wheels a cart piled high with bodies past the barracks. I see that some of the bodies still have shoes, so I run out and say, "I don't have any clogs to…"

"Go ahead," he says, motioning to the pile of bodies.

I find a pair that fits me and am now able to walk through the snow without my feet freezing.

When Taty returns that evening and hears about the doctor, he is not surprised. Nothing surprises us anymore. "Well," he says, "he could have killed you. You're still alive. You'll be fine."

He's right—over the next several days, he helps me change the bandages on my neck, and within two weeks, the wound has healed.

The months pass and the snow becomes less and less frequent. When it does come down, it clings to the ground for only a few hours before the sun burns it away. The days grow longer. Fleets of aircraft pass high overhead more frequently. There is no more work for us, and we begin to see panic on the guards' faces.

One afternoon, as we are marched from the barracks, a man approaches me and says, "Alec? Is that you?"

When I look at his face, I recognize him as a man my family knew in Tarnobrzeg.

"Alec, I've just seen your brother Yitzchak. He arrived two days ago from Rzesców and is being held in barracks 15, the recuperation barracks. He isn't well, Alec. You must see him."

For the first time in longer than I can remember, I feel something other than hunger inside. For the past year, Taty and I have wondered about Yitzchak and Mamy and Channah. Now my brother is here, in the same camp we are.

I run to barracks 15 and when I enter I see that the bunks are nearly empty. All of the men are out marching or have been taken out for an execution. Only a few are scattered here and there, covered in blankets, too weak to move.

"Yitzchak! Yitzchak!" I yell. None of the men stir.

I climb to the top bunks and lift the blankets covering each person I can see. The first is an old man. The next is the same. I jump down to the next level of bunks and continue looking.

"Yitzchak! Yitzchak!"

I climb down one more level and lift the blankets from the next person I see. The man is a skeleton, but I can see in the shadows that he is younger than the others. I strain to find more of the details in his face, which is bruised and swollen. Rivers of dried blood stain his nose and ears. But beneath it all, I see my brother.

"Yitzchak! It's me, Alec."

He struggles to turn his head towards me. When his eyes reach me, he lets out a whisper of words—"Alec—my brother Alec." Tears form in his eyes. "Alec—I don't think I'll make it much longer. I can't even stand on my own. Here," he reaches slowly under his body and removes a small piece of bread, "take this. You must eat and survive."

"What happened to you, Yitzchak?"

"One of the kapos clubbed me when I arrived. I can no longer eat. I'm not going to make it."

I feel tears on my face. I am looking at my brother, who belongs with Taty and me. I want to pick him up and carry him back to be with us. I want to find rations for him and help him get better. But I cannot carry him to our barracks. There is no food to be found. There is nothing I can do. Nothing.

"Hold on, Yitzchak, this won't last much longer. We'll be free soon."

"Alec," he says, "if one of us doesn't make it, the other has to try to find Mamy and Channah. Promise me that, Alec."

"I promise, Yitzchak."

He closes his eyes and is silent.

"I have to go. I'll be back early tomorrow. Hold on, Yitzchak."

I pull the cover over his head and run back to tell Taty, who is shocked when he hears the news. "Yitzchak? My son Yitzchak? Are you sure? You see, I told you he's alive. Maybe Mamy and Channah are as well. I have to see him."

But there is no way for him to go to the barracks now. One of the guards will surely see him and question him about where he is headed. Or worse.

"I'll go back tomorrow to check on him," I say. "Maybe you can see him later on."

In the morning, before roll call, the square is busy with men lining up for bread, and I am able to sneak out to see Yitzchak again. I run to

Yitzchak's bunk and pull the cover from his head. The face that stares up at me is not his. It's that of an older man. I look at the bunk to make sure I'm where I saw Yitzchak yesterday.

"Did you see the man who was here before you?" I ask the man.

"No," he says. "I just arrived, and it was empty."

I jump down from the bunk. "Yitzchak! Yitzchak!" I run to the toilet, which is where the dead are piled for the body collectors every morning. On the floor are three bodies. I turn them over and look at each of their faces. But no Yitzchak.

I don't know what to do or where else to look. He couldn't be dead. He was alive only hours ago. I told him to hang on, that the war would be over soon, that I would be back to see him. He has to be alive.

In the distance, at the entrance to one of the crematoria, I see two body collectors working on their cart, which is piled high with corpses.

I run towards them.

As I get closer, I see them removing the large straps that hold the dead prisoners in place. They are preparing to dump them onto a metal slide that leads down to the incinerators. I get closer and closer to them as I run, but before I can get to them, I watch as they lift the handles of the carts and send the bodies sliding down and away. By the time I arrive, they are gone.

Something tells me that Yitzchak was with them.

When Taty hears that Yitzchak is gone, he refuses to give up hope. "Did you see his body?"

"No."

"Then he may still be here somewhere."

It is only several days later that Taty begins to realize that Yitzchak is gone. "If he were here and still alive, he would come to look for us," he says. At night, I hear him repeating Yitzchak's name over and over: "Yitzchak, Yitzchak, my son, wherever you are, I hope we'll be together soon. And then we'll tailor and be with Mamy and Channah and Alec, together again as a family."

Spring has arrived, and the guards are more anxious and worried than ever. Work has been replaced with endless marching and roll calls.

One morning, we pass by the jail and can see an execution taking place in the small yard behind. Several men are marched out past Nazi guards on their way to the gallows. One has been beaten so badly that his nose seems to have been torn off; another is naked except for a pair of glasses. At the base of the scaffold, the naked man stops and prays before climbing the stairs to the nooses. He is calm, walking as though he is going to meet an old friend. Even as the Nazi officers shout at him, he is at peace.

I see both men drop just as our group passes from view.

Days later, when we are assembled in the courtyard, we stand waiting for hours. The guards meet in small groups for hushed conversations with each other, then disperse to other small groups. None of them seem to know what to do next.

Finally, one of them makes an announcement: "You will march to the train station."

We march several miles to the station, where we see a train waiting for us. Soldiers order us onto open-top boxcars and the train pulls out. We travel for several hours before we begin to hear a strange noise over the sound of the train. The sound grows louder and louder until we can no longer hear the train's engine, which is only a few cars ahead.

My mind races to place the sound—a loud wailing noise that sounds almost like a siren that grows louder and louder by the second. The train slows to a stop and the howling of the siren increases until it begins to hurt my ears. Then, over the siren, we hear explosions and feel something hammering against the car, followed by the splintering and shredding of the wooden walls that surround us. The explosions pass over us and we can hear them continuing on the car in front of us, then the sound of exploding metal on the locomotive.

Overhead, the sirens turn into the sound of low-flying aircraft, which fly so close that we duck as they pass.

"It's the Americans," the men around us begin saying. "The end is finally here."

I glance around and see that the gunfire has killed many of the men in our car, but no one seems to notice. Many are trying to climb up to the top of the car to look outside. Two men help to lift me up to the top of the wall. I hook my arms over the top to hold myself up and look out. The planes dive for another look at the train, but they do not fire this time. One passes directly overhead, close enough for me to see the tiger mouth painted on its nose, the machine guns mounted in its wings, and the pilot in the cockpit.

Their gunfire has torn the boxcars apart, but when I look at the train's engine, I see that the planes weren't after us—smoke is pouring out of hundreds of holes in the locomotive and the conductor hangs half inside and half outside his window.

We sit on the damaged train until the next day, when we hear the sound of another train approaching from up ahead. When it appears, we see that it's a single engine that the German soldiers work furiously to couple with the destroyed locomotive. Once attached, the new locomotive moves us for another hour before we hear the sound of diving aircraft once again. We stop just as a group of six passes overhead, firing their machine guns into our car and the new locomotive. The gunfire stops and a single plane passes over, followed quickly by an enormous explosion. The men lift me up once again, and just as I reach the top of the car, another plane passes, dropping a dark object from its belly. An explosion louder than the first nearly knocks me down, and when the smoke begins to clear, I can see the tracks ahead of us standing straight up in the air in a twisted mess.

The door opens again and frantic soldiers order us out. Taty and I jump to the ground and crawl under the train. Many follow us. Others run to ditches on either side of the tracks. We hear the planes coming in for another attack and see the Nazi soldiers drop to the ground with their machine guns. The screaming of the planes grows closer and we hear their machine guns firing and the ground around us explodes as the bullets fall. We hear them hammering into the car above us, the tracks, the locomotive. The planes pass over and we survey the damage around us. I can see that several of the bullets have pierced the thick iron rails of the track. A Nazi guard near us never gets up from the ground—his neck has been destroyed by one of the bullets.

"He's going to hell without a stop," Taty says.

Another prisoner says, "What the Nazis don't kill, the Americans will."

Soldiers order us from the ditches and from under the train, and we stand awaiting roll call, but it doesn't come. The officers stand nervously holding their machine guns and searching the sky for any sign of approaching aircraft. Several prisoners take advantage of the soldiers' preoccupation and run out to the surrounding fields to dig for potato seedlings. When they return, many others surround them to take advantage of the feast.

The soldiers return and order us to line up again, but before they can begin counting, a commanding officer says, "We have no time to count. We'll take what we have and leave the rest. Check their hands and mouths for dirt—if they've been eating potatoes, shoot them."

We are ordered to hold out our hands for inspections. Those who have been out in the fields are taken away from our view. Moments later, we hear the crack of pistol fire and only the soldiers return.

"No more trains for these subhumans," the commanding officer announces. "They're going to walk. They'll stay in the woods during the day and march during the night. We can't expose them to the public."

9.

April 1945
The Death March

More than six hundred of us are marched into the nearby woods, where we sit and wait, guarded by a hundred or more soldiers. Evening comes, bringing rain and sleet. Taty and I huddle together for warmth. We haven't eaten since before leaving Flossenbürg, but there's no use thinking of this—the only food around sits on a wooden horse cart that several prisoners are ordered to pull. Only the soldiers eat.

When darkness is upon us, we are ordered up and begin marching single-file in the mud and freezing rain. Men fall behind, exhausted, and minutes later we hear the crack of rifle fire.

At daybreak, we are ordered back into the forest where we collapse from the night of marching. Those who have the energy to wonder ask, "What now? Where are they taking us?"

"They're probably trying to find a way to do away with us."

Taty listens, then turns to me and says, "I wonder if the Americans will ever get to us."

Overhead, we hear the drone of aircraft, and when we look up through the trees we see low flying planes. They bank and circle over us until we hear a massive explosion on the ground. Our eyes follow the sound and see the wagon that carries all of the soldiers' food and ammunition in flames. The soldiers run frantically around it, trying to control the fire before all is lost. But it is no use. Their ammunition begins popping and exploding inside the flames and they are forced to back away and stare into the fire.

"What will they do now, without food and ammunition? How much longer can it last?" someone says.

The cart burns for hours. I fall asleep and am awakened throughout the day by the commotion of the soldiers, who huddle together in conversation. Artillery explosions echo around us, and we begin to see unarmed soldiers running through the forest, as if they are being chased by some dangerous animal. They run past the soldiers overseeing us without stopping.

Night comes and we are ordered to our feet. We march through the freezing night until dawn comes and we collapse once again in the forest. Sleep comes more quickly now, and I begin dreaming of marching and rifle fire and explosions. We are awakened and march, then sleep, then march. I lose track of how many days it has been since we left Flossenbürg, but I can see that the starvation and exhaustion are taking their toll. Men drift in larger groups back to the end, towards a line of soldiers waiting for them with their rifles. Some simply drift to the side of the road and sit down to rest. The soldiers are quick to follow and execute all of them.

Taty is growing weaker by the minute. He begins to drag his feet and shuffle along like an old man. His face and eyelids are swollen, as are his feet and ankles. "If there ever was a hell on earth, the Nazis have made it even worse," he says. Then, "If all the oceans, the lakes, the rivers, the ponds in the world were to be transformed into ink, they would run dry in a short time recording the Nazis' atrocities." I can tell he is weary, delirious. We begin to fall behind, and I know what will happen if this keeps up.

I look behind us every few minutes to make sure we are not approaching the back of the line. I put my arm around Taty's waist to help him along, knowing that if he stops, there's nothing I can do.

Daybreak comes again and we see the dark outline of a barn in the distance. We are ordered inside, where we collapse once again. Every hour or so, solders enter and take three prisoners outside. We hear three shots and know that our time is coming.

Later in the morning, I look out through the barn's open doors and see a nicely dressed woman approaching the soldiers carrying a bucket filled with something. She reaches into the bucket, removes an object, and begins to toss it towards us. I can see it's a steamed potato and suddenly become aware of the emptiness in my stomach. But before it leaves her hand, one of the soldiers approaches her and puts his pistol to her head.

"How dare you try to feed these subhumans!"

The woman stops but seems unafraid of the pistol: "These are men; they're not pigs."

"You're right, they're not pigs," the soldier says. "They're less than pigs."

She drops the bucket and the potato in her hand, reaches into her apron, and removes a small black book, which she waves in the soldier's face. "Do you see this Bible?—This will cure it all!"

She holds the book in his face for a moment before picking up the bucket and heading off. The officer lowers his pistol and goes back to converse with the rest of the soldiers.

Night falls again, but tonight we do not march. We shiver in the freezing darkness, hoping that sleep will come to relieve us from the cold and hunger. Every few minutes, we are awakened by soldiers entering and taking small groups of men outside. We always know how many they take by the number of gunshots we hear after they leave.

Morning comes and we are awakened to shouting soldiers ordering us outside. When I try to get up, I feel that my shirt is frozen to the ground, and I have to carefully pry it loose. Those of us who are left line up outside and watch silently as the soldiers huddle once again for a hushed conversation. They seem to have no idea what to do with us.

They converse until a young boy appears on the road. He is not one of us—he's clean and well fed, and he stops at the soldiers, who halt their conversation and stare down at him.

"I was just in the town square," he says, "and the Americans are here!"

"Where is the square?" one of the soldiers asks. "How far?"

"It's just down the road," he says, then runs off.

The soldiers turn to each other for a moment. Surprisingly, they drop their weapons and packs and run off to save themselves.

For several minutes we stand silently in line, staring at their packs. Men look at each other without saying a word. Others collapse. Several guard dogs run around frantically, trailing their leashes, searching for their handlers. But for several moments, the Nazis still control us.

Then, just as quickly as the soldiers disappeared, one of us finally steps out of line and runs off. Others follow him, and the line disappears in waves. Some men simply sit down, others go back to the barn. There is no celebrating, no embracing.

"We need to go in the opposite direction of those soldiers," Taty says. He grabs my arm and leads me down the road, which is wet and muddy from the rain that fell last night. We come to an embankment and climb up, away from the road, to wait. On the way up, Taty finds an abandoned pack containing several pounds of dried noodles. "I'll keep this," he says. "We'll find water and eat."

As we sit, waiting, we hear the rumble of engines in the distance, and minutes later a military vehicle appears. It has wheels on the front and tank treads on the back and several soldiers march next to it, some with Americans flags on their uniforms, others with Czech flags. They see us and wave us down.

When we reach them, they look at us until one of the Czech soldiers begins to weep and says, "How can someone do this to people?"

No one answers.

They help us inside the vehicle and take us into town. "I think we're going to be fine," Taty says, as if he is commenting about the color of the officers' uniforms. There is no emotion in his voice, no elation or excitement. I cannot feel these emotions either. We have simply left the barn and the other prisoners, we've been picked up by another group of soldiers, we are still hungry and wondering about the rest of our family. Nothing has changed.

We arrive at a hospital in the town of Neunburg vorm Wald, where we are given beds with clean sheets. Just before I drift off to sleep, I look over at Taty. He is already fast asleep, his head resting not on the pillow, but on the backpack filled with noodles.

10.

After the War

When I awaken, I think I'm dreaming. It's quiet and I'm in a bed with clean sheets. Nuns wearing black habits and robes pass by the foot of my bed, moving in all different directions, stopping at patients to deliver medicine and food. I look to my right and see Taty still sleeping with the bag of noodles under his head, and then I remember the barn, the Nazis running, the soldiers who found us. In the bed to my left is a former prisoner with blood-soaked bandages covering what seems to be a large wound near his chin.

A nun sees that I am awake and comes towards me with a tray of food. When she smiles at me I realize that this is the first compassionate face I've seen in many years.

The tray is filled with more food than I can remember seeing in one place and at one time—potatoes, vegetables, small pieces of meat. I want to eat it all, but I swallow only a few bites before my stomach begins contorting and I vomit.

"*Nein! Nein!* Why are you throwing up?—this is good food," she says.

"I can't eat. It won't stay down."

"Let's try something else, then."

She goes away and comes back with mashed potatoes mixed with cream and butter. It smells wonderful, but when I swallow it comes up immediately. I look to the nun and see worry on her face: "You can't digest food. I'll get a doctor right away."

She returns with an army doctor who examines me. He's Jewish and speaks to me in Yiddish: "I've never seen someone as skinny as you are. Wait here a minute. I'll be right back."

He returns with two other doctors, and they confer with him until the Jewish doctor speaks again. "I think you'll pull through. You're just bones covered with skin now, but if you stay away from meat and fats, you'll get stronger."

"But what can I eat, then?"

"I'll figure something out for you. Don't worry."

Hours later, he returns, finds one of the nuns, and brings her into the kitchen. When they emerge, he walks to my bed and sets a tray down in front of me.

"I've ordered the nuns to make this for you whenever you need it. It's rice and diluted powdered milk. You should be able to digest it. But promise me you'll eat it as often as possible."

I make the promise. As soon as he leaves, I take several bites and wait for the food to come back up just like the rest did. But it doesn't—this time, it stays down.

"You see, Alec, there is a God to look out after us," Taty says. He has just awakened and is eating his food without any problems.

I eat the rice and powdered milk for weeks before the nuns begin feeding me small portions of ground beef. The taste of the meat is awful and I complain. One of the nuns takes the beef away and comes back with the same tray. It seems as though it's the exact same food. "Try this," she says.

I taste the meat again and smile. When I look at her, she says one word: "Garlic."

For the next two months, I eat the beef and garlic, until the nuns finally start feeding me normal meals. When they're not bringing me and the other patients meals, they're constantly changing bedding to control the lice that we brought in from the camps. Before we're allowed back in our beds, they dust the new sheets with a white powder that helps control the insects.

Several more months pass by—exactly how many I cannot say. I've gained enough strength and weight to satisfy the doctors, and Taty, who has recovered quickly, says, "It's been eleven months, Tulek. Maybe it's time for us to leave the hospital. I can find work as a tailor in town."

Eleven months. It's enough to convince me that he's right. It's time to move on.

Taty tells the nuns that we're ready to leave, and a short time later, two U.S. Army MPs show up at our bedside to tell us they've made living arrangements for us in town. We follow them outside to 1 1/4 Austrasse Street, a two-story house in a quiet neighborhood.

When the MPs knock on the door, a woman in her sixties answers.

"Mrs. Rossman?" one of the MPs says.

"Yes?"

"A room in your house has been requisitioned for these two survivors—Samuel and Alec Mutz. They'll be staying with you until further notice."

"Oh, please, please, come in. I'll be happy to cook and clean your bedding for you."

Inside, she shows us to a room on the second floor. "You'll stay here. There are two beds for you, and again, I'll change your bedding for you. Come down for dinner at noon."

Taty and I rest for several hours before we go downstairs for supper. Mrs. Rossman is standing over a large pot that sits on the stove. "Help yourself. I made chicken soup for you."

Taty looks into the soup and sees something that he doesn't like. He moves his face closer to the pot and peers inside. "Mrs. Rossman," he says, "I see some strange things floating in your soup. Did you clean the chicken before you put it into the soup?"

"Of course I cleaned the chicken—I removed all of its feathers."

"But did you clean out the bird's stomach? Did you remove its intestines?"

Mrs. Rossman looks suddenly embarrassed: "No."

We are silent for a moment until Taty laughs. "Well, thanks for the effort, but let me cook the chicken from now on."

Taty has no trouble finding work the next day, and before long, we begin searching for Mother and Channah. We walk to the town square every morning, where a large billboard is filled with notices of people searching for relatives, with notes containing names of survivors in other towns. A small crowd gathers here every day and trades clues back and forth. Taty mostly listens, until he hears someone mention Dębica or

Tarnobrzeg. "Tarnobrzeg? Did you say Tarnobrzeg? Have you seen my wife, Necha Mutz? Or my daughter, Channah Mutz? We last saw them at selection near Dębica."

The answer is always no, yet we always walk to the square hopeful. Perhaps this will be the day. But we leave without answers, and after months of listening and asking, I begin to think that they are gone. Still, we awaken each morning and follow the same ritual of following vague rumors that lead us nowhere.

1946 turns to 1947 and there is still no news of Mother and Channah. Taty puts his pillow on the windowsill every morning to air it out, and every morning I can see that it is wet—soaked through as if someone poured water over his face in the middle of the night.

It takes me months before I finally ask him: "Taty, why is your pillow wet every morning?"

His head sinks and he suddenly seems smaller. "Those are my tears for your mother and Channah."

He turns and leaves the room for the walk to the town square.

It is 1948. While he never says it, I can see Taty is beginning to accept that there's no one left. He writes my aunt Liftcha—Mamy's sister—in New York, asking if I can stay with her. "There's nothing left for you here, Alec," he says. "We need to go to America. You need to grow and learn. And you can't grow here."

He asks around and finds an old World War One veteran who is willing to teach me math, history and, most importantly, English. His name is Dr. Reitinger, and he walks on a wooden peg leg. Much of our time together is spent talking about his experiences—serving with the German army during World War One, being drafted to serve with the Nazis at the age of sixty-five, then being dismissed when they saw his fake leg. But in between stories of his life, he presents me with information on every subject I can imagine, and I devour it all. Food, it turns out, is not the only thing I was deprived of during the war.

After several months, Dr. Reitinger is impressed with my progress. "You're a fast learner," he says.

By the time Taty receives a response from Aunt Liftcha, I am confident with my English and with my other subjects. After he reads the letter, he says, "Our relatives in America are anxious to see us. But you need to go over first. I'll follow in several months."

"No!" I say. "We need to stay together."

"Alec, you're her blood relative. I'm not. It would be too much for both of us to show up at the same time. Trust me."

Only days later, my bag is packed and I'm standing with Taty at the station, waiting for the train to Bamberg, where I'll go to the American consulate for paperwork. When the train arrives, I turn to Taty and break down. He is my only family. I think of all we've been through together and sob uncontrollably at the thought of leaving him.

"Don't worry, Tulek, I'll see you soon."

I find my seat on the train and look out the window at Taty. As the train begins moving, I think of that day when we watched from the truck as Mother and Channah faded away. And now, years later, I watch as the last living member of my family disappears into the distance.

11.

A New Life

The train stops in Bamberg, where I walk to the American consulate for an examination. They ask questions about my health and my relatives in New York before examining me and giving me the OK to continue on. I board another train for the city of Bremen, where I am examined again and told to wait for the next available ship. A week later, an Army transport ship arrives and we are ordered to board.

When I get to the dock, I am shocked by the boat's size. It's larger than all of the buildings I've seen in my life put together. It towers overheard, and when I look down its length, I cannot see where it ends.

There are hundreds of survivors like me on board, and we immediately begin introducing ourselves and conversing about where we were imprisoned, where we grew up, where we were liberated, how many of our family members survived. Many I speak with are just like me—their families have been wiped out and they are joining relatives in the United States.

I stand on the deck and watch as a team of men wrestle with the giant ropes holding the ship to the dock. Then tugboats push us out and we head towards the open ocean.

Eleven days later, in the early morning darkness, we approach New York City. Those of us who are awake are on deck, watching as the thin strand of lights in the distance grows larger and the details of the city begin to reveal themselves. Soon, the lights have grown to take up the entire horizon, and then we see them lift off the water and take the forms of skyscrapers and bridges. I see a road with a steady stream of headlights flowing into and out of the city. I never imagined that so many cars existed in all the world.

As morning comes, I see the outline of buildings that rise into the clouds, and I wonder how anyone can bear working so high up.

Two tugboats meet our ship and guide us into the docks, where the ship is secured and the gangplank lowered. We gather our possessions and are called off the ship, then directed to uniformed customs officials who stand with folded arms waiting for us.

"Name?"

"Alec Mutz."

"Country of origin?"

"Poland."

"And what are you bringing into the country?"

"My belongings."

The official opens my bag and catches the stench of my clothing, then quickly closes it. "Good enough—continue on."

I walk just beyond the customs table to a crowd of people, many of whom are carrying signs with the names of family members they're waiting to meet. I search the signs until I see a woman holding one with my name printed on it.

"I am Alec Mutz," I say to the woman. "Are you Aunt Liftcha?"

"Alec!" she says. "Welcome to America. No, no—I'm not your aunt. I'm from the organization that sponsored your immigration. Your aunt is waiting for you just over here. Follow me."

She takes me to a group of three women and a man, all of whom smile when they see me. The women look nothing like my mother, but I assume they're her sisters. They hug me and examine me from head to toe. "Alec? Alec! Welcome to New York. Oh—what a good looking young man you are," one says before turning to the other. "Can you believe what a good looking young man he is?"

"Thank you," I say.

"Oh, and he speaks such good English," the other says. "I'm your Aunt Liftcha, and this is your Aunt Hentcha. And this is your cousin Lilly and her husband Harry."

"Hello. It's very nice to meet you."

"Follow us to the car. We'll take you to our apartment," Liftcha says.

We walk under an elevated train on our way to the car, and I wonder why anyone would build a railroad above the ground. It doesn't make sense to have one over people's heads. There are signs everywhere—billboards with advertisements for Macy's, the Ford Motor Company, Coca-Cola. I want to stop to read every single one of them. I could spend days looking at them and I still wouldn't come close to reading them all.

"Here we are," Liftcha says. Her husband Harry unlocks the door of a brand-new Buick Roadmaster—a massive, gleaming automobile. It's the biggest car I've ever seen. As I climb into the back seat, I think that these people must be rich New Yorkers to afford such a wonderful car.

We drive from 23rd Street to 14th Street, and my eyes are glued to the windows for the entire ride. Thousands of people cross the streets, hail taxi cabs, carry bags of goods from shop to shop. We pass an enormous sign that reads "Klein's," and Liftcha says, "You can buy any kind of clothes you'd like in that store."

She turns and hands me a long, yellow object. "You must be starving. Here—have a banana."

I have never in my life seen a banana, but I know from what she said that this must be some kind of food. I open my mouth to take a bite, but she stops me just as my teeth are about to sink into the yellow skin.

"No! No! You don't eat the peel. Here, give it to me for a moment."

She peels the fruit and hands it back to me. "There, now you can eat it just fine."

I've never tasted fruit quite like it before. It certainly tastes nothing like the blueberries that grow back home. But it feels good in my stomach, so I finish eating it and roll down the window to dispose of the peel. We're stopped at a traffic light, and a police officer is standing on the corner.

"No! No! Don't throw it out the window. Don't you see that police officer? He'll give you a ticket if you do that."

"A ticket?" I say. This makes no sense to me. My English teacher taught me that a ticket is something you buy to go to the cinema. Why would a police officer give me a ticket for throwing a banana peel out the window?

Liftcha sees my confusion. "You'd get a *fine*. If a police officer gives you a ticket, you have to pay a fine. It's not the same as a ticket to the circus."

I hand her the banana peel and roll up the window. I have a lot of things to learn.

After we arrive at Liftcha's apartment and I'm shown around, she brings me into a room and becomes very serious. "Alec, why didn't your mother, brother, and sister survive?"

"I don't know," I say.

"Did you look for them?"

"Yes—we looked for years."

"How did you look? Are you sure there isn't a chance they're still alive?"

"We asked around—people who saw them, people who also had relatives waiting in the field at Dębica. Those who didn't go to labor camps were taken away to be killed."

She lowers her head and pauses. "Why didn't they live, Alec? Why couldn't they have survived like you and your father?"

It's a question I've asked myself every day since Taty and I began slowly realizing we'd never see them again. And up until now I've never been able to answer it. But here, in New York City, in the apartment of one of the last links I have to my mother, the question somehow sounds different, and I give her the best answer I can—"They were in the wrong place at the wrong time."

EPILOGUE

Because I came to the United States with the intention of being a permanent citizen, I was required to register for the draft. Liftcha took me to the draft board in 1949. Shortly after that, I got my first job at a pawn shop on 8th Avenue and forgot about the draft altogether.

In 1950, Taty arrived from Germany. He hated New York from the start—the noise, the buildings, the lack of land and fields and quiet. He stayed for five months before deciding to go back to Germany. But shortly after returning to Europe, I received a letter from him. "There is nothing left for me here. It's been cold and rainy for days. The mud is ankle deep."

I wrote back: "The sun is shining in New York. The weather is pleasant here. Why don't you come back?"

On Thanksgiving Day, we heard a knock on the door. And there was Taty.

Aunt Liftcha's apartment was too small for the two of us, so we found our own apartment a few blocks away. Taty found work quickly as a tailor and hated every minute of it. It was mass-production work, the emphasis on quantity, not quality. He approached the shop owner several times to protest: "These jackets we're making are of poor quality. They'll fall apart in no time. I want to do the stitching my way."

The owner was never interested in hearing Taty's complaints or putting up with his stubbornness. If he didn't like the work, he told Taty, he could quit. There were plenty of tailors who would be willing to take his place.

Taty stayed.

He struggled, too, with communication. His English was so poor that he often had trouble reading signs and labels. One evening, I returned home from work and asked him if we had anything for dinner. "Yes, yes," he said, "I went to the market and bought some canned food. It tasted strange, but I left some of it in the refrigerator for you."

When I opened the refrigerator I saw the opened can of food.

"Taty, this is dog food. You shouldn't be eating this. Didn't you see the picture of the dog on the label?" I said in Polish.

"Yes, yes, I saw it. But I saw a woman putting several cans of it into her basket. I thought it would be all right."

"She was probably buying it for her pet, not for her family."

We had a good laugh, then went to the task of finding a suitable meal for the evening.

It was during meals, more than any other time, that Taty and I would talk about Mamy. No matter where we were, Taty would take a taste of the food and lean in close to tell me how Mamy would have cooked the same meal, which herbs she would have used, what it would have looked like when served.

In 1952, I received a notice from the draft board instructing me to report to 39 Whitehall Street at five next morning. I was devastated. I had only just arrived in this country, had just gotten a job, and was just beginning to settle in. My family was gone and all the horrors of war were fresh in my mind. And now I was being told to join the army. Why, I wondered, did all these things have to happen to me?

But there was nothing I could do. I packed my bag, said my goodbyes, and headed for the subway on the day I was to report. The man at the turnstile looked at me and said, "Aha—I know where you're going. Lots of guys like you heading off this morning."

"I wish I knew where I was going," I said.

"You'll be all right," the man said. "Army'll treat you well. Good luck."

From the subway we were loaded onto busses for Camp Kilmore, then onto new busses and the Aberdeen Proving Grounds, where we were given uniforms, boots, dog tags. When I received my tags, I noticed a small notch in the edge and asked why it was there. "That's so when you die, we can stick your tags in your mouth. The notch is for your teeth—it holds your mouth open. Now move along!"

Basic training was difficult. Where most of the men struggled with the physical part of the training, I struggled with the language. It seemed every one of our instructors had a heavy southern accent. My English was good, but their speech sounded to me like a different language. March training always began with us in straight lines, the drill sergeant shouting a strange command: "*Let…let…let…let…let… let.*" At first I had no idea what he meant, but I figured it out when I saw the men around me lifting their left legs in time with the officer's commands.

Then there were the commands that everyone seemed to understand but me: "Drop down and give me twenty-five, Mutz."

I had no idea what he wanted me to give him, or what "dropping down" had to do with it. *Twenty-five?* Twenty-five what? The only thing I could think of that people asked for was twenty-five cents, so I reached into my pocket and removed a quarter.

The drill sergeant's face grew crimson. "You kiddin' me, Mutz? You kiddin' me? Bein' a funny man?" He turned and gave the same command to the man next to me, who dropped to the ground immediately and started pushups. "That's what I want, Mutz—now give me twenty-five!"

After basic training, I was trained at a small-arms school, where I spent four months learning how to disassemble, clean, reassemble, and repair just about every firearm the army used. Then I received my orders. I was to be shipped overseas, but I was not yet told where, only to report back to Camp Kilmore to await transport.

At Kilmore, I heard that I was being shipped to Germany to serve. They loaded us onto a train, then onto a massive transport ship. As we pushed out to sea, I thought of arriving in New York for the first time. This time, I watched the Statue of Liberty fade away and thought of the notch in my dog tags and wondered, "Will I ever see the Statue of Liberty again?"

Ten days after setting off, we arrived in Germany and were transported to Replacement Depot Sandhofen, a German barracks that still bore the swastika and other markings of the Nazi war machine. I was not happy. To me, the Germans could not be trusted.

Two weeks later, we reported to the flagpole with our belongings, where we received our next orders. I was to report to Nellingen Air Force Base. "You're to be a goodwill ambassador," the commanding officer told me.

I served at Nellingen for a year. During the winter of 1952, I received leave and was able to visit Neunburg and the house Taty and I stayed at after we were released from the hospital. Mrs. Rossman answered the door and at first had no idea who I was. She saw the uniform, then studied my face for what seemed an eternity. "Alec? Alec! Alec is here—unbelievable. How is America, Alec? Come in, come in."

I visited for several hours, during which I answered all of her questions about our life in America. Her questions were easy until she got to the one I wasn't expecting: "And when did the rest of your family join you, Alec?"

"They didn't join us, Mrs. Rossman. They were all killed."

"Oh," she said, "I'm very sorry."

Not long after I returned to base, I was called into the commanding officer's office. "I was told you speak German and Russian," he said. "The Russians are forming satellite armies in Latvia, Estonia, Lithuania, and God knows where else. We need to counter this by training Germans how to use American weapons. Since you speak German, I need you to lead the training process."

I thought of Mother, Channah, Yitzchak, Grandpa Wolf, the starving and the beaten, the German soldiers who met us at every train station and had their fun by firing into the barracks at Wieliczka.

"No—I'm not going to do that."

The commanding officer sat back in his chair, shocked. "What? Do you realize that I can have you court-martialed for not following my orders?"

"I realize this, yes."

"And are you going to tell me why you will not follow these orders?"

"No, I'm not."

He stared at me for some time before he said, "You're dismissed." That was the last I heard from him.

My service in the army ended in 1954 and I returned to New York City. A year later, one of my friends gave me a girl's number. "I went out on a date with her," he said. "She's a very nice girl, but I'm so short that she had to wear low shoes for dancing. It wouldn't work out with us. Her name is Phyllis. You should give her a call."

I did.

That weekend, Phyllis and I went to Camaratos, a restaurant in the Bronx, for dinner and dancing. We dated several times after that and kept in touch while I was attending college hundreds of miles away at the Rochester Institute of Technology, where I was studying printing.

We married in 1957. Phyllis's father bought us a car, which we packed full of our belongings for the long trip from New York to Rochester, where I had a job waiting for me at Kodak. Two flat tires and many, many hours later, we arrived and began settling in our new apartment.

Our lives took off very quickly after that. Our children began to arrive in 1962, with our son Andy. A year later our second son, Mitchell, arrived. Then in 1971, our daughter Nancy. Taty remained in New York City, where he settled into a routine of tailoring, listening to music, and visiting us regularly. By the time the boys began heading off to college in the early 1980s, Taty had become ill and moved up from New York City. Together, we found him a small apartment just down the road from us in Brighton. We saw each other almost every day, and he came to the house several times a week for dinner.

In 1980, he went to the hospital after his illness worsened. After numerous tests, he was diagnosed with cancer of the large intestine. Surgery to remove part of his intestine was successful, but he never fully recovered. He told me on several occasions that he felt he was a burden on our family. No matter how hard I tried to convince him otherwise, he continued to believe this.

He died in 1981, at the age of eighty-five. I still miss him very much.

In 1988 I was contacted by the German Consulate of New York City and asked to serve as a witness to the prosecution for a trial against Commandant Schwammberger, from Camp Mielec. I traveled to New York in June, where I was interviewed by both the German prosecutor and Schwammberger's defense attorney. They asked me to tell them everything I knew about the commandant's day-to-day actions in Camp Mielec. I told them everything I knew—about his saying, "I am your God. If I say you die, you die" to prisoners before executing them, about pushing the man into the electrified fence. I told them about the prisoner who looked Schwammberger in the face as he walked by, about what the commandant said just before murdering the man: "You looked in my eyes, you filthy Jew swine. You don't look in God's eyes." I told them about how he nodded approvingly as two guards tortured the prisoner who stole the potato.

My son Mitchell was working as a musician in Stuttgart, Germany when the trial began, and he updated me as often as he could. In the end, Schwammberger received a life sentence without parole. He only served several years of the sentence before being diagnosed with Alzheimer's disease. His attorney asked the court to commute his sentence, but the court told him to reapply at the age of one hundred. Schwammberger died not longer after, at the age of 92. There is no punishment in the world that this man didn't deserve. Taty was right when he said that Nazis like Schwammberger made hell on earth. This man deserved to die in prison. And while I am proud to have played a role in his trial, nothing can be done to bring back the thousands of people who died because of his actions.

After my retirement from Kodak in 1993, I began reading a great deal about the Holocaust, including accounts of life at Flossenbürg. I wanted to understand what it was that caused the loss of so many lives, what it was about the Nazis that made them do the things they did to Mamy, Channah, Yitzchak, and the millions of others like them. It was in one of these books that I came across a description of the execution of Admiral Wilhelm Canaris, a Nazi officer who plotted to assassinate Hitler, and Pastor Dietrich Bonehoffer, a religious leader who was an outspoken opponent of the Nazi Party. Both men were executed at Flossenbürg, just before the death march began. Admiral Canaris, according to the accounts I read, was badly beaten before he was led to the gallows wearing what remained of his uniform. Pastor Bonehoffer was stripped naked and walked to the gallows wearing only his glasses. Witnesses say that he was peaceful as he ascended the gallows, at one point stopping for what seemed a silent prayer before they hanged him. As I read accounts of these executions, I remembered the execution I witnessed as we marched by the jailhouse, just before they put us on the trains to leave the camp. I believe the men we saw being hanged that day were Canaris and Bonehoffer.

I returned to Flossenbürg with Mitchell in 1995, fifty years after we were liberated. We traveled in a bus with other survivors from around the world. We visited the train station where Taty and I were unloaded, the stairs that the soldiers forced us to march up and down, the barracks where the soldiers stayed. We participated in ceremonies commemorating the camp's liberation. The mayor of the town, who was a boy when we were liberated, gave an emotional speech during which he apologized for the Nazis' atrocities. At one point, an old woman in a wheel chair was brought in to see us. She was grateful that we had returned, and after a few minutes many of us recognized her as the woman who tried to throw potatoes to us just before the soldiers put down their weapons and ran.

I've spent a great deal of time over the years thinking about my life in the military, about how frustrated I was when I received that initial draft notice. My service in the United States Army was difficult, but the longer I wore the uniform, the prouder I became. And now, many years later, I am even prouder still. I often think back to our last months in Flossenbürg. I remember U.S. Army soldiers overseeing the exhumation of victims from mass graves simply so that those victims could receive some semblance of a proper burial. And I remember my condition when that army truck picked us up after the Flossenbürg death march. I weighed sixty-seven pounds and wouldn't have made it much longer had the United States military not arrived. They were responsible for restoring my soul and my life. I am honored to have worn the same uniform as those who saved me.

In 1998, my wife and I were flown to Washington, D.C. , to a ceremony at the Capitol Rotunda honoring me and other survivors of the Holocaust. I sat next to Congresswoman Louise Slaughter and listened to speeches from some of the most important people in Washington. As I sat there, I thought of how far I had come in life. There I was, a Polish immigrant who so nearly became one of the more than 1.5 million children to perish during the Holocaust; the son of a tailor from the small town of Tarnobrzeg, Poland, being honored in front of Congress at the Capitol Rotunda in Washington, D.C. It was one of the proudest moments of my life.

Nothing, however, makes me prouder than when Phyllis and I get together with our family. Andy, Mitchell, and Nancy are all highly educated. They have married wonderful people and given us seven wonderful grandchildren. As I watched our children grow up, I often wondered what things would have been like if the Nazis never interrupted my life. I'm sure my family would have stayed in Poland, where Yitzchak might have taken over Taty's shop. Channah might have gone to university and become a scholar. Mamy and Taty might have grown very old together.

Just before this book was sent off for publication, I contacted the United States Holocaust Memorial Museum in Washington, D.C., hoping that their research staff would be able to tell me exactly what happened to Mother and Channah. Taty and I once heard that the women and children who remained in that field near Dębica were loaded onto trains and taken to Belzec for extermination. But we never knew for sure. In 2007, the Museum gained access to millions of Holocaust documents available through the International Tracing Service, located in Bad Arolsen, Germany. My hope was that researchers at the museum would be able to locate documentation of Mother's and Channah's fate.

After several months, I was contacted by one of the head researchers and told that his search had turned up record of neither my mother nor my sister. His explanation for this was simple: There was no reason for the Germans to waste time documenting every woman and child destined for the death camps.

The ITS did, however, contain documentation of Taty, Yitzchak, and me. Most of what remains amounts to simple forms indicating our names, approximate dates of birth, religion, and prisoner numbers. One form lists me as having been executed on April 22, 1945. It also states that my body had been exhumed shortly after the war's end. I was amused by this form—I had no idea that I had died and come back to life.

Sharing my experiences with audiences is still difficult. Speaking about my survival transports me back in time, where I am once again in Taty's shop, watching from behind the curtain as the Nazis threaten to cut his belly open. Or again in the back of the truck with Taty, watching as Mother and Channah fade away. Or staring into Yitzchak's beaten face and running frantically to find him after he was removed from the barracks. Each time I relive my experience, I take weeks to recover.

But it is important for me to tell my story. It is impossible for people to understand what the destruction of six million people means. They need to see a face, to ask questions. I worry about what will happen when these faces are all gone, when the questions can no longer be answered by people who were there to witness the Nazis' atrocities firsthand.

Not long ago, I had a young high school student approach me and ask to see my tattoo. When I showed her my wrist and the crude "KL" tattooed on it, she looked at it in disbelief. "Can I touch it?" she asked.

"Sure—it's real."

She rubbed it with her finger, half expecting it to come off. When it remained, she seemed satisfied.

This is why I tell my story.

APPENDIX I

Timeline of Events

1930: Alec Mutz born in Tarnobrzeg, Poland

1938: Nazi Germany annexes Austria

September 1, 1939: Nazis invade Poland

September 17, 1939: Nazis enter Tarnobrzeg

October 1939: Tarnobrzeg's Jews ordered to Radomysl, Poland

December 1939: Mutz family joins family in Mielec, Poland

February 1941: Mutz family returns to Tarnobrzeg

June 1942: Nazis order Tarnobrzeg's remaining Jewish citizens
to Dębica, Poland;
Necha and Channah Mutz sent to Belzec extermination
camp;
Yitzchak separated from family and sent to labor camp;
Alec and Samuel sent to Rabbi's sanctuary, Tarnobrzeg

June 1943: Alec and Samuel taken to Camp Mielec

July 1944: Transferred to Camp Wieliczka

August 1944: Transferred to Camp Flossenburg

April 1945: Alec sees Yitzchak for the last time in Flossenburg

April 14, 1945: Flossenburg Death March begins

April 23, 1945: Camp Flossenburg liberated

May 8, 1945: War in Europe ends

June 1949: Alec arrives in New York

APPENDIX II

Mutz Family Tree

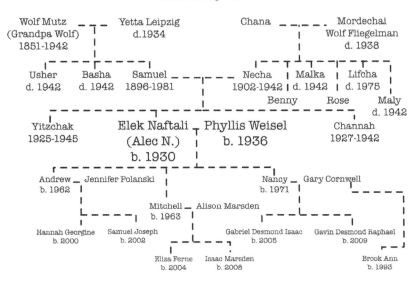

Wolf Mutz — — — Yetta Leipzig   Chana — —,— — . Mordechai
(Grandpa Wolf)   d.1934   Wolf Fliegelman
1851-1942   d. 1938

Usher   Basha   Samuel — — —,— — Necha | Malka | Lifcha
d. 1942   d. 1942   1896-1981   1902-1942 | d. 1942 | d. 1975
                                                    Benny   Rose   Maly
                                                                                  d. 1942

Yitzchak   Elek Naftali — Phyllis Weisel   Channah
1925-1945   (Alec N.)   b. 1936   1927-1942
                  b. 1930

Andrew — Jennifer Polanski   Nancy — Gary Cornwell
b. 1962   b. 1971

                Mitchell — Alison Marsden
                  b. 1963

Hannah Georgine   Samuel Joseph   Gabriel Desmond Isaac   Gavin Desmond Raphael
b. 2000   b. 2002   b. 2005   b. 2009

                Eliza Ferne   Isaac Marsden   Brook Ann
                b. 2004   b. 2008   b. 1993

ACKNOWLEDGEMENTS

I must thank the many people who have helped make this book a reality.

Haley Blanchette, Alicia Charland, Emily Cirincione, Jeanie and Alexandra Grimm, Mary Hydar, Sam Martina, Rebecca Moore, Madison Osgood, and Keith Pedzich all read and provided feedback on the rough draft. Many of the suggestions they offered helped the book take its final shape.

Xioaping Hung spent countless hours transcribing recorded conversations about my experiences.

Kevin Stewart illustrated the family tree, timeline, and map of Europe.

My children Mitchell, Andy, and Nancy offered their feedback on the final draft and encouraged me along the way.

My wife Phyllis suggested the title and helped me with some of the details. She has been a source of support throughout the project (and for the last fifty-three years of marriage).

And, finally, to Dr. Peter Marchant, who many years ago invited me to speak in his Literature of the Holocaust class at SUNY Brockport and first brought up the possibility of writing a book. Our many hours of conversation about my life in Poland later turned into an early draft. Without him, this book would never have happened.